GW01079945

Little Laureates

Verses From Surrey
Edited by Michelle Afford

First published in Great Britain in 2007 by:
Young Writers
Remus House
Coltsfoot Drive
Peterborough
PE2 9JX
Telephone: 01733 890066
Website: www.youngwriters.co.uk

SB ISBN 978-1 84431 266 5

Foreword

Young Writers was established in 1991 and has been passionately devoted to the promotion of reading and writing in children and young adults ever since. The quest continues today. Young Writers remains as committed to the nurturing of poetic and literary talent as ever.

This year's Young Writers competition has proven as vibrant and dynamic as ever and we are delighted to present a showcase of the best poetry from across the UK and in some cases overseas. Each poem has been selected from a wealth of *Little Laureates* entries before ultimately being published in this, our sixteenth primary school poetry series.

Once again, we have been supremely impressed by the overall quality of the entries we have received. The imagination, energy and creativity which has gone into each young writer's entry made choosing the poems a challenging and often difficult but ultimately hugely rewarding task - the general high standard of the work submitted ensured this opportunity to bring their poetry to a larger appreciative audience.

We sincerely hope you are pleased with this final collection and that you will enjoy *Little Laureates Verses From Surrey* for many years to come.

Contents

Thomas Donnelly (11)   16
Lauren D'Costa (11)   16
Fergus Tanner (11)   17
Rebecca Furlong (11)   17

Oakhyrst Grange School
Stephanie Lindo (11)   18
Emily Ruiz (11)   18
Miranda Batki-Braun (11)   19
Georgina Candy (11)   19
James Kemp (11)   20
Sam Bushell (11)   20
Adam Giles (11)   21
James Hall (11)   21
Callum English (10)   22
Aaron Boorman (11)   22
James Male (10)   22
Katharina Jungclaussen (10)   23
Millie Hopkins (10)   23
Christy Welsh (10)   24
Grace Udale (9)   24
Josephine Niemira (9)   25
Benedict Malby (9)   25
Christopher Latchem (9)   26
Benjamin Donohoe (10)   26
Lauren Rose (9)   27
Matthew Day (9)   27
Adam Stoneman (10)   28
Emily Little (9)   28
Thomas Dawson (8)   28
Blanche Brown (8)   29
Lauren Giles (8)   29
Oliver Clarke (8)   30
Aman Mahi (8)   30
Michael Doble (8)   31
Rebekah Lindo (9)   31
Aimée Dyer (8)   32
Jack Bushell (8)   32
Stefan Harper (7)   33
Sam Lefevre (9)   33
Holly Macbeth (7)   34

Parish Church Junior School

Billy Thompson (10)	53
Sarah Langhorne (10)	53
Heather Gibbs (10)	53
Hannah Mwebeiha (9)	54
Machaela Prendergast (10)	54
Tommy Marsh (10)	55
Tameka Gowan (9)	55
Susan Mohammed (10)	55
Krystal Clark (10)	56
Hannah-May Reid (10)	56
Charlie Coker (10)	57
Malaika Nwankpa (10)	57
Laurence Ben Johnston (10)	58
Joshua Aidan Elliott (10)	59
Hadjer Boumazouna (9)	59
Kenya Barnett (9)	60
Rhianna Rock (10)	60
Aaron Bennett-Jordan (10)	61

Parkside School

Sonny Cott (10)	61
Michael Woolston (9)	62
Oliver Mould (10)	63
Oskar Kolk (10)	63
Ben King (10)	63
Charles Hibbert (10)	64
Harrison Lee (10)	64
William Payne (10)	65
Louis Broomfield (9)	65
Andrew Howorth (9)	66
Edward Grove (10)	66
Oliver Haines (10)	67
Renny Smith (10)	68
Oliver Dunn (10)	68
Max Kerslake (11)	69
Charlie Crook (9)	69
Adam Welby (10)	70
Dominic Wood (10)	71
Harrison Moore (10)	72
Freddie King (10)	72
Christopher Addison (11)	73

Alex O'Brien (10)   73
Charlie Horne (11)   74
James Hibbert (11)   74
Matthew Szepietowski (11)   75
Harris Asher (11)   75
Brian Ryu (11)   76
Nicolas Stolz (11)   76
Hugo Solway (11)   77
Oscar Ferguson (10)   77
Brandon Koen (10)   78

St Hilary's School, Godalming
Julia Parison (11)   79

St Hugh of Lincoln Catholic Primary School, Woking
Michael Griffin (9)   80
Michael Chapman (9)   80
Emily Bullen (9)   80
Megan Louise Avery (8)   81
Sophie Hubbard (9)   81
Daniel Naughton (8)   81
Charlie Ruiz (8)   82
Georgia Quigley (9)   82
Thomas Vardy (8)   82
Niall Runswick (9)   83
Alice Ketteringham (9)   83
Alyssa Charlotte Promnitz (9)   83
Samuel Robinson (8)   84
Rory Kelly (9)   84
Estelle Harland (8)   84
Niamh Ryan (9)   85
Billy Peacock (8)   85
Isabela Maria Ramanath (8)   85
Aimee Cook (8)   86
Connor McLean (9)   86
Joshua Jones (9)   86
Aoife Coyle (10)   87
Adam Hayton (10)   87
Anastasia Murphy (9)   87
Elliot Samuels (10)   88
Allyson Varndell (10)   88

Charlie Kaine (10)	88
Chloe Foster (10)	89
Hannah Randall (10)	89
Jasmine White (10)	89
Ella De Vivo (9)	90
Jaime Miranda (10)	90
Ryan Fernandez (10)	90
Alexander Frow (9)	91
Darius Mohepat (10)	91
Sophie Stevens (10)	92
Katie Naughton (10)	92
Jay Mearns (10)	92
Nicola Turner (10)	93
Charlie Watson (9)	93
Thomas Buckland (10)	93
Shannon Phillips (10)	94
Georgia Blanco-Litchfield (10)	94
Sophie Cawkwell (10)	94
Isabel Turner (11)	95
Thomas Ketteringham (11)	95
Emma Higgins (10)	96
Emily Randall (11)	96
Rosie Byers (11)	97
Samantha Love (11)	97
Daniel McNulty (11)	98
Ciara Sullivan (10)	98
Emma Cooper (11)	99
Ryan Quigley (11)	99
Ellen Verrier (10)	100
Alice Langley (11)	100
Nicola Hayes (11)	101
Reece Power (11)	101
Jessica Martino (11)	102
Stephen Frangiamore (11)	102
Alex De Piano (11)	103
Charlotte Smith (11)	104
Nicholas Haley (10)	104
Hannah Baron (11)	105
Hannah Brierley (10)	106
Terry Dullaghan (11)	106
Kevin Heath (11)	

South Farnham Junior School

The Chandler CE Junior School

The Poems

Autumn Morning

Slowly, the sun starts to rise over the huge green land,
Slowly, you start to open your hand,
Slowly, the slugs start to slide,
Slowly, the birds get out of their nests and start to sing and glide,
Slowly, the turtle starts to walk,
Slowly, the people start to talk,
Slowly, the fruit starts to grow,
Slowly, the baby cygnet turns into a swan.

Paige Hunt (10)
Devonshire Primary School

Friends Forever?

I cause commotion because
My best friend's filled with emotion.
No, she shan't and shall never be
My friend forever.

She's the only friend I've got,
That's why I like her a lot.
Should she never
Be my friend forever?

She's the loveliest,
But also the closest.
She can't and will never
Be my friend forever.

I know she's dying
And I am crying.
Should she never ever,
Be my friend forever?

Elsa Jerlija (10)
Devonshire Primary School

One Scary Night

I was startled by a frightened cry,
Probably a dream, that is why,
But no - then I heard it again,
I got out of bed and checked the den.

Suddenly a big fat giant came storming out,
The monster had an enormous snout,
Then the thing leapt at me,
I quickly dived, lucky I was free!

I ran away as fast as I could,
It followed me, I thought it would,
Found a police box - dialled 999,
The police came rushing, just on time.

Policemen surrounded the big thing,
Guns were all they could bring.
They shot down the monster,
All that was left was laughter.

Kavitha Appulingam (11)
Devonshire Primary School

Silence

(Based on 'A Poem to be Spoken Silently' by Pie Corbett)

It was so quiet
I heard an ice lolly melt.

It was so quiet
I heard a gemstone scream.

It was so quiet
I heard a diamond sing.

It was so quiet
I heard a cookie crumble.

It was so quiet
I heard a tree die.

Laila Howard (10)
Devonshire Primary School

The Shadow

It was a full moon,
There were lots of shiny, glimmering stars.
I went downstairs to get a drink,
Suddenly I looked at the grandfather clock.
Emerging out of nowhere, a shiny figure appeared
And flew across the clock, as quick as a bolt of lightning.
I was shocked.
My water shot out of my hand.
I was horrified.

I realised that the figure went upstairs.
Quickly I raced up the stairs,
Trying not to wake up anyone,
Even though we had some really creaky floorboards.

All at once I cornered him,
Then I had a good look at him.
He had scary bulging eyes, a huge mouth and had a tiny body;
And then he vanished through the walls and left no trace.

Heather Underwood (9)
Devonshire Primary School

Midnight Archer

The midnight archer gallops to a destination,
A destination unknown to everyone.
He rides with fear and desperation,
To a land beneath the blazing sun.

The midnight horse whinnies whilst carrying the archer,
With hooves of lead and thighs like rock,
With a heart of sheer darkness
It rides throughout the land.

The archer is as dark as a crow,
But as white as snow as he illuminates.
He will disappear forever with the sun upon his back.
Fiery sun release the secrets of the archer.

William Hardy (10)
Devonshire Primary School

Eternity's End

The rain descending down from the heavens,
Splintering onto the jagged, snowy peaks.

Meteorites breaking into shards as they enter the Earth's
cloudy atmosphere,
Causing massive scars on our planet.

The trees blowing violently in the destructive wind,
As their leaves fly off silently into the distance.

The birds take flight as their flawless wings take the to the skies.

Humans heeding the call to their deaths as the volcanoes erupt,
Creating pools of lava, blazing holes, incinerating all in their path.
Tsunamis flooding cities and beaches, wrecking everything
but themselves.

At last the Earth, being crushed by all that is being thrown at it,
The blistering heat from the lava has incinerated holes through
the Earth's flesh.
The fiery pits of Hell have been unleashed upon the world.

The raging tides sweeping up everything that is even close to them.

The life on Earth, crusading to the mountains,
Thinking it will help them, even though it won't.

Finally the Earth is destroyed after its pain and sorrow.

Connor Nolan (11)
Devonshire Primary School

Night

Night, a shadowy phantom in the darkness,
Eyes that children dare not look at.
His black cape creeps to every corner of the Earth.

With his long silver nails he scratches the stars into the sky,
His endlessly long hair whips the moon into place.
He fights with the sun and loses again,
He goes back to his palace of darkness and shame.

Joshua Hall (11)
Devonshire Primary School

The Owl

Why do you have big wings with feathers like the blackness
of the night
and eyes as bright as the moon?
Why do you have wings that carry you as fast as a speeding light?
Why do you catch your prey like a shooting star?

Jacqueline Morgan (9)
Devonshire Primary School

Pets

Having a pet is a wonderful thing,
It's amazing what joy puppies can bring.
But: cats, dogs, birds and hamsters too,
Always need caring for by me and you.

Agnieszka Kowalska (11)
Devonshire Primary School

Autumn

Coats come out as it gets colder,
Leaves are orange and brown.

Rain begins to come our way,
We stay inside throughout the day.

Flowers begin to fade away,
Ready to pop out in spring one day.

We get prepared as winter dawns,
To cut the hedges and mow the lawns.

Megan Jones-Dellaportas (10)
Devonshire Primary School

My Magic Box

(Based on 'Magic Box' by Kit Wright)

I will put in my box . . .

Thundering words that say hello,
Waves swishing on ice-cold snow.

I will decorate my box . . .

With gold and silvery, cold ice
And put my brother on breezy snow.

I will put in my box . . .

A dog and a cat barking mad,
Scratching walls like paper flaps.

I will put in my box . . .

A dragon freezing cold,
Breathing snow instead of burning fire.

I will put in my box . . .

My family and my brother
Playing with my father and my mother.

Keith De Jesus (9)
Devonshire Primary School

As Loud As . . .

As loud as thunder crashing in the wind.
As loud as a rocket blasting into space.
As loud as an aeroplane zooming off to take
                                    people to an airport.
As loud as a laptop with funky, funky, funky music.
As loud as a bumblebee when it is laying eggs.
As loud as a trumpet when someone is playing it.
As loud as a nursery with loads of toddlers.

Tia Catlin (9)
Green Wrythe Primary School

As Sad As . . .

As sad as a puppy with no one to stroke it.
As sad as a book with no one to read it.
As sad as a cat with no one to pet it.
As sad as paper with no one to draw on it.
As sad as a baby with no one to care for it.
As sad as a pencil with no one to write with it.
As sad as a house with no one to live in it.
As sad as a diary with no one to use it.
As sad as a hat with no one to wear it.
As sad as a bird with nowhere to fly to.
As sad as a boy with no one to play with.
As sad as gold with no one to take it.
As sad as the sea with no one to swim in it.
As sad as a clown with no one to laugh at him.
As sad as a game with no one to play it.
As sad as a skateboard with no one to ride it.

Sam Wagstaff (9)
Green Wrythe Primary School

As Sad As . . .

As sad as a rocket with no one to fly it.
As sad as a pocket with no one to sew it.
As sad as a poor Miss Sikingley.
As sad as a door with no one to paint it.
As sad as a dog with no one to wash it.
As sad as a tear with no one to sew it.
As sad as a cake with no one to eat it.
As sad as a desert with no one to walk it.
As sad as a kitten with no one to stroke it.
As sad as a cup with no one to win it.
As sad as a car with no one to drive it.
As sad as a volcano with no one to light it.

Cameron Borthron (8)
Green Wrythe Primary School

As Sad As . . .

As sad as a lonely tear.
As sad as a puppy with no one to stroke it.
As sad as a promise and someone has broken it.
As sad as a sock with no one to wash it.
As sad as an orphan with no mum and dad.
As sad as a toy that a bully has broken.
As sad as a book with no one to read it.
As sad as a teddy with no one to cuddle it.
As sad as a building with a crane that's broken down.
As sad as pencil with no one to use it.
As sad as a bookmark with no one to use it.
As sad as a girl whose heart has been broken.
As sad as a boy with no friend to play with.
As sad as a door when someone has broken it.
As sad as a squashed bug.
As sad as an ice cream with no one to lick it.

Jordan Brooks (8)
Green Wrythe Primary School

As Sad As . . .

As sad as a teddy with no one to cuddle it.
As sad as an odd sock never to be washed.
As sad as a tear on its own.
As sad as a mouse that has no cheese.
As sad as a volcano never to erupt.
As sad as a baby with no mother to care for it.
As sad as a promise to be broken.
As sad as a book that hasn't been read.
As sad as a pyramid with no one in it.
As sad as Egypt with nothing in it.
As sad as old clothes never to be worn.

Janie Newell (8)
Green Wrythe Primary School

As Strong As . . .

As strong as King Kong flexing his muscles.
As strong as a dinosaur crunching Brussels.
As strong as a bug waiting to kill.
As strong as an ox who is willing and will.
As strong as a gorilla swinging through the trees.
As strong as the Hulk crawling on his knees.
As strong as a sword breaking rock.
As strong as a boxer willing to box.
As strong as an aeroplane flying through the sky.
As strong as a mountain way up high.
As strong as a monkey swinging through the trees.
As strong as a tap turning out the water.
As strong as a lion charging people
As strong as a man smashing cars.
As strong as a gun waiting to kill people.
As strong as King Kong picking a car up.
As strong as the Hulk running up the wall.
As strong as a computer playing games.
As strong as a dog fighting with a cat.
As strong as a table hard to snap.
As strong as a leopard fighting a gorilla.
As strong as a sea lion bursting out of the water.

Ben Taylor Honey (8)
Green Wrythe Primary School

As Sad As . . .

As sad as a puppy with no one to stroke it.
As sad as a kitten with no one to hug it.
As sad as a hamster with no one to feed it.
As sad as a baby with no one to care for it.
As sad as a girl with no one to play with.

Lauren Fanciulli (9)
Green Wrythe Primary School

As Fast As . . .

As fast as a rocket going up into space.
As fast as me winning the race.
As fast as a racing car *zoom-zoom-zooming*.
As fast as a cheetah who is looming.
As fast as an aeroplane taking off at the runway.
As fast as a motorbike driving to the motorway.

Jamie Rowlinson (8)
Green Wrythe Primary School

As Lonely As . . .

As lonely as a hard ruler.
As lonely as a furry kitten.
As lonely as a puppy feeling very ill.
As lonely as someone with no mum or dad.
As lonely as a bottle being kicked.
As lonely as a book with no one to read it.
As lonely as a pencil with no one to use it.
As lonely as a teddy with no one to cuddle it.
As lonely as a laptop with no one to use it.
As lonely as a baby with no mum or dad.
As lonely as me with no one to love me.

Abbie Lumsden (9)
Green Wrythe Primary School

As Sad As Me

As sad as a book not being read.
As sad as a child in an orphanage with no family.
As sad as a homeless baby.
As sad as a lonely teardrop.

Lewis Scott (9)
Green Wrythe Primary School

Some Loud Stuff

As loud as a big dragon roaring loudly.
As loud as a bell ringing high.
As loud as a huge triangle tinkling out loud.
As loud as a small drum pumping up.
As loud as a terrifying tiger!
As loud as a teacher shouting!
As loud as a girl screaming.
As loud as a nursery bubbling.
As loud as a big bird screeching.
As loud as a storm thundering.
As loud as a glass breaking.
As loud as an engine with no petrol in it!

Jessica Holland (8)
Green Wrythe Primary School

As Sad As . . .

As sad as a dog with no one to stroke it.
As sad as a tear running down someone's face.
As sad as a cow with no one to milk it.
As sad as a Miss Sikingley with no one to teach.
As sad as a teddy with no one to care.
As sad as a mouse with nothing to eat.
As sad as a baby with no mother to care for it.
As sad as a bed with no one to sleep in it.
As sad as a pyramid with no pharaoh in it.
As sad as an egg with no one to eat it.
As sad as a pharaoh who's only just died.

Stuart Morgan (8)
Green Wrythe Primary School

Joy

If joy was a colour it would be a bright yellow like the centre
of the Earth.
It would look like a ball jumping up and down in the sky.
It would sound like a quick, snappy tune that comes from the circus.

Joy smells like a steaming hot mince pie on Christmas morning.
The touch of joy is a never-ending circle.
It feels like you are sitting by the beach all hot and sticky;
Then you go into the cold salty seawater to cool off.
Joy makes me feel like bouncing around, singing merrily.

Miles Whicher (11)
Laleham Lea Primary School

Joy

Joy's colour is bright yellow, swirling around, hoping to be
gathered up to make the world a better place.
It looks like a monkey jumping from tree to tree, swinging freely
in the jungle.
Joy sounds like shouts of happiness, escaping from fun times.
It tastes like chocolate melting and sliding on your tongue,
or Coca-Cola fizzing in your mouth.
My joy feels like warm furry slippers and fluffy sheep,
where you could get lost in their deep curls.
It smells like incense burning in front of you, wafting through you.
It makes you feel life is exciting and fun.

Joseph Brockman (10)
Laleham Lea Primary School

Sadness

The colour of sadness is a light blue just like the tip of an icicle.
The sight of it is a dull boy doing absolutely nothing.
It tastes like a sour onion going to make your eyes pop out.
The touch of it would be when someone puts their hand through
your body.
The smell of it would be from the fridge in which something
is decaying.
The feel of it makes me weary and very tired.

Sean Rickell (11)
Laleham Lea Primary School

Laziness

Laziness is like a wonderful sparkling green in the bright stars.
It is relaxing in front of the television with your eyes glued to it.
Your mum nagging you to do your chores but you hear just
blah, blah, blah!
It's like stuffing your face with sweets.
It feels like you are lying on a soft and comfy cloud.
It smells like a luscious roast dinner with lovely steaming gravy.
It feels like I will never do chores again.

Jonathan Downer (11)
Laleham Lea Primary School

Happiness

Happiness is full of love and joy.
It sounds like a dove flapping its wings in the air.
It looks like the wind brushing through the flowers' leaves.
It's like the sweet taste of bees' yummy honey swirling
down your throat.
It's like a cosy touch of a fleece that has just been made for you.
It's like the sweet, sweet, sweet smell of a new, fresh beginning.
Happiness makes me spill all my love and joy.

James Ganley (10)
Laleham Lea Primary School

Anger

Anger is a swirling mixture of a deep, cold black,
     twisting around a furious, scorching red.
It looks like a bomb ticking away ready to explode and attack.
A devil is scrambling around, deviously trying to get out.
Anger sounds like vigorous explosions
     and ear-splitting cracks.
You can hear the steam sizzling out of your ears.
As bitter as horseradish punching you in the stomach.
Anger feels like a hot, stinging pain,
     like a needle piercing your flesh.
The smell wants to make you faint, it's putrid.
Your body shivers all over as you breathe in the scent.
You feel surrounded by fire that will not be extinguished.
Your stomach is filled with a non-stop roller coaster churning your
     insides.
As your brain stops and your heart turns off, the rage takes over your
     body and the hatred inside you grows *even bigger!*

Duncan Kavanagh (11)
Laleham Lea Primary School

Anger

Anger is a fiery red.
It feels hot and burning.
It's tall and fierce,
And takes control with its ear-splitting
    roar that kicks and beats, punching inside you.
It tastes hot and spicy.
It burns and scorches, boiling up inside you,
     ready to burst.
It smells raw and meaty, dragging you in.

Molly O'Shea (11)
Laleham Lea Primary School

Joy

Joy feels like the waves swiftly but silently hitting the cliffs.
It is the mixture of many colours, all bright and exciting.
It is the exotic smell of fruits all sweet and sour.
It is the wonderful sight of the Australian coastline sizzling
                    with the beautiful reef not far below.
It is a freezing cold ice cream sundae with swirling cream and a
                                    cherry on the top.
It is the sound of a million birds twittering in the trees.
It is the touch of a furry, cuddly kitten.
It feels like a dream that has finally come true.

Mairead Jackson (11)
Laleham Lea Primary School

Guilt

Guilt is like an everlasting black, getting heavier and heavier
                    with every step.
It's like the never-ending image of a man trying to sleep but too
                    full up with painful thoughts.
'Tell the truth!' chant the voices in the brain of the lonely, guilty
                    lad's head.
It tastes of bitter mould getting bigger and bigger, hour by hour.
When you touch it, it feels like your hand is being shoved into
                    an endless pile of wet, slushy snow.
Its smell is of moaning and groaning.
The inside of your nostrils is prickly with it
It feels like a giant hole eating into you.
Like a blowtorch burning its way through a sheet of metal.

Liam Murphy (11)
Laleham Lea Primary School

Happiness

Happiness is like a very light blue duck's egg.
It looks like a playful, bouncy ball that soars high above your head.
Like an eagle racing to the stars in a sapphire blaze.
Happiness feels like a powerful energy, quickly filling you with
hope and dreams.
It tastes like fresh grapes bursting with juice, just begging
to be eaten.
Happiness sounds like a group of people laughing and joking.
Happiness smells like a plump Christmas turkey wafting its
scent over the table.
Calling everyone to come and eat.

Thomas Donnelly (11)
Laleham Lea Primary School

Happiness

Happiness is a soft, gentle touch that lights up your world.
It looks like a white dove elegantly flying through the magnificent
morning breeze.
It smells like a rose churning up your nose, spreading your body
with eager happiness.
It tastes like a succulent cherry filling your heart with a glorious
and sugary taste.
It feels like a newborn kitten's fur, soft as snow, light as a feather.
It reminds me of a pair of playful puppies cuddling up to each other.
It's like a set of peachy, luxurious cushions.

Lauren D'Costa (11)
Laleham Lea Primary School

Guilt

Guilt is the colour of a pale cream that would blind you every time
you fear.
Guilt looks like a black shadow of a roaring giant that points his huge
finger at you.
Guilt sounds like people screeching in your ear.
Guilt tastes like mouldy apples being shoved down your throat.
Guilt feels like a rough serrated knife that cuts the toughest bread
but really it's cutting your heart.
Guilt smells of burning pain and horror damaging your insides.
Guilt makes you feel like a tiny person thrown into the corner of a
freezing cold prison cell.

Fergus Tanner (11)
Laleham Lea Primary School

Sadness

Sadness is a dull grey that you can't stop seeing.
It looks like dead flowers, drooping and crumpled up,
                whilst others are bright and cheerful.
It sounds like the soft, painful moaning of millions of people
                echoing in your ears.
It is the taste of the sourest food in the world sticking in your throat.
It feels like a heavy weight, pushing you down to the floor.
It smells like a salty sea that you can't escape from.
Sadness makes you feel that you may as well give up trying
                to be happy.

The whole world is against you.

Rebecca Furlong (11)
Laleham Lea Primary School

The Environment

Water, water flowing in the sea
How many rubbish cans can you see?
Trees, trees swaying in the air
Is there still CFC up there?

The ozone layer around the Earth,
Was the hole there when I had my birth?
How many whales can you see?
To be precise, there's only 350.

So now you see what is happening to the Earth,
Please help me save it before my child's birth.
We can make a difference to the world
And we can make it now!

Stephanie Lindo (11)
Oakhyrst Grange School

Rubbish

Rubbish, rubbish everywhere,
There's so much here I'm pulling my hair.
Global warming, what a shame
People ruining this world again and again.

The ozone layer, what a fuss
People dissing it like a load of dust.
Sometimes I think they really don't care
And what will happen to the polar bears?

One day the world will not exist,
Then where will we live?

Emily Ruiz (11)
Oakhyrst Grange School

My Brother

Well my brother is my brother,
And he's as *brotherish* as can be!
Sometimes I love him,
But only when he's nice to me.

Sometimes when he's horrible,
I scream . . . or go and tell Mum,
Or go inside my room and sob,
And get my homework done.

Well my brother is my brother,
He's a nice kind of guy,
And he will always be my brother,
'Til the day I die.

Miranda Batki-Braun (11)
Oakhyrst Grange School

A Night Hunter

She stalks the animals angrily, her eyes gleaming bright,
She watches the stars carefully, that twinkle in the night.
She purrs softly and gently when she catches her prey,
Then off she runs in search of more, there's no time to stay.
She sneaks through the grass and claws up the trees,
And catches so playfully the leaves in the breeze.
She runs around her territory, making sure all is intact,
Then off she runs again in search of mice and rats.
As the sun slowly rises in the eastern sky,
The hunter slowly fades away, fades away to die.
But when the sun puts itself to bed and the clouds fill with rain,
My little cat Millie becomes a fearful hunter again.

Georgina Candy (11)
Oakhyrst Grange School

Rubbish Day

On Tuesday I take out the rubbish,
The stink makes me feel funny.
It attracts flies,
The stench floats around in the sky
But sometimes I forget,
I get told off before I make an excuse.
But next time I take out the rubbish,
I'll remember to hold my nose to stop me feeling funny.

James Kemp (11)
Oakhyrst Grange School

Bobby Star

There once was a little car
Whose name was Bobby Star.
He was loved by his owner
But Bobby was just a loner.

He longed for just one mate
And would wait at his owner's gate,
For a drive around the town
But not having friends did get him down.

He decided not to mope
As he rolled down the slope,
His handbrake had gone wrong,
Bobby went faster as he went along.

He had never gone this fast before,
The other cars shouted as they saw
Bobby stopping at the bottom of the hill,
Thank goodness, at last he was still.

The other cars now thought he was cool
And no longer ignored him like a fool.
He's now know as Bobby Star,
The really cool fast car.

Sam Bushell (11)
Oakhyrst Grange School

Age Difference

The Children

Playing football,
Watching TV,
PlayStation 2
And PSP.

The Teenagers

Hanging around,
Texting friends,
Growing up starts
But childhood ends.

The Men

The young children
Are now men
And the cycle of life
Goes round again.

Adam Giles (11)
Oakhyrst Grange School

My Doodles

I like to doodle,
Doodling is fun
I like to doodle for everyone.

I like to doodle
Poodles and noodles
Sometimes even apple strudels.

I like to doodle
Until the sun goes down
And I like to doodle all over the town.

One day I doodled on my teacher's bag
Then she got really mad.
So now my doodling days are done
But while it lasted it was fun.

James Hall (11)
Oakhyrst Grange School

Sports Oh Sports

Cricket is cool but sometimes boring,
Football is fun, especially when I'm scoring.
Boxing is dangerous and very violent,
People watching tennis are very silent.

Ice hockey is played with a stick and a puck,
And it's fun to play rugby in the muck.
Swimming is tiring and very wet,
Netball involves shooting balls into a net.

In badminton you use a very light racquet,
The best thing with a squash ball is to whack it.
Sport keeps you healthy and is great fun,
You can play with your friends in the rain and the sun.

Callum English (10)
Oakhyrst Grange School

My Dog Sheba

My dog Sheba has fleas and wobbly knees,
My dog Sheba likes balls and cotton wool,
My dog Sheba likes going on walks,
(Did I tell you, she can talk?)
My dog Sheba really likes to bark,
But, *no, no, no!* She doesn't like the dark.
But most of all . . .
Sheba is my dog!

Aaron Boorman (11)
Oakhyrst Grange School

Sea Of Blue - Haiku

There's a sea of blue
Those cheery little bluebells
Swaying in the breeze.

James Male (10)
Oakhyrst Grange School

In The Spring Field

The aeroplane is buzzing around,
Daisies and bluebells on the ground.
Children playing on the mound,
Hear the children's hearts while they pound
With all the running around.
Paths in the shadows that people have found,
Children laughing all around,
This is spring, I'm bound!

Katharina Jungclaussen (10)
Oakhyrst Grange School

The Spring Flowers

Flowers are big,
Flowers are small,
Flowers are nice,
Flowers are cool.

Some are purple,
Some are white.
Bees and wasps.
What are they?
Friends to flowers.

Flowers are pretty,
Flowers are beautiful,
Flowers are lovely,
Flowers are colourful.

Some are yellow,
Some are blue,
You look around,
And no doubt you'll see a *flower!*

Millie Hopkins (10)
Oakhyrst Grange School

What Spring Brings

Clouds drift over the ground,
Bluebells all around.
Little birds sing in little voices,
I hear a plane and other noises.

The green, green grass,
The dew that looks like glass.
The daisies, the sunflowers,
Strong sun which gives them powers.

I hear the trees rustle,
Tussle, hustle, bustle.
The leaves are dark green, light green,
Many shades in-between.

When the day comes to die,
I let out a great big sigh.
You know what they say,
Tomorrow is another day.

Christy Welsh (10)
Oakhyrst Grange School

Beautiful Bluebells

Beautiful bluebells all purple and blue,
Everywhere I walk there's a carpet of blue.
The sun shines brightly in the sky,
I hope my bluebells never die.
Now I look up to the sky,
And watch the clouds floating by!

Grace Udale (9)
Oakhyrst Grange School

Spring Flowers

See the golden daffodils,
Swaying in the breeze.
See the pretty pink blossom,
Growing wildly on the trees.

The white and yellow daisies,
White specks amongst the grass.
Now the pretty tulips
All have bloomed at last.

See the sapphire bluebells,
An ocean of green and blue.
See a pretty sunflower
Turn to face the sun.
See a pretty sunflower,
Now the day is done.

Josephine Niemira (9)
Oakhyrst Grange School

Spring Bluebells

B luebells are calm, soft blue,
L ike the tropical sea.
U p, towering in the breeze,
E nding in the sky.
B luebells come out in spring,
E veryone shout 'Hooray'.
L ike a painting
L ike the sky,
S ing out loud 'Bluebells'!

Benedict Malby (9)
Oakhyrst Grange School

Bluebells In Spring

B lue as the morning sky
L ike a sea of azure
U nlike any other flower
E verywhere
B eautiful
E xtravaganza
L uxurious blue
L ike a carpet over the land
S even thousand of them to love.

I nviting
N o field without them.

S pringing from the ground
P resenting themselves to their audience
R ain helps them grow
I nfiltrating the garden
N othing's more beautiful
G rowing through the world.

Christopher Latchem (9)
Oakhyrst Grange School

Spring

S pring has come, let's go outside,
P laying on the shiny slide.
R avenous wasps come out to sting,
I love the beautiful spring.
N othing's better than the longer days,
G rowing flowers and the fields of maize.

Benjamin Donohoe (10)
Oakhyrst Grange School

Leaves

F ull of gladness
A way they fly
L oving loveliness in my eye
L ong, short, fat, thin
I n the woods, and all around
N eutral colours on them I found,
'G aze up,' said everyone.

L eaves drop on the floor,
E verywhere they are, oh yes
A ll are leaves are they not?
V ery pretty
E veryone look
S o tonight I will dream, about falling leaves.

Lauren Rose (9)
Oakhyrst Grange School

Spring In Surrey

Spring in Surrey, what could be better?
A long time ago it used to be wetter.
The flowers and the plants, what a delight,
From hibernation, the birds take flight.

The leaves on a tree, in the warm breeze,
Enjoying the views, falling on my knees.
Spring in Surrey, the best sight I've seen,
I hope it doesn't change because it's nice, warm and green.

The animals and the bees, isn't it great?
What a great day, there's nothing I hate.

Matthew Day (9)
Oakhyrst Grange School

Nature

Nature is here to make us happy,
It sometimes makes babies wet their nappy.
It makes people want to play,
Every night and every day.
Nature is here to make us cheerful.

All the creatures are here,
It sometimes makes us cheer.
The sun shines to make plants grow,
So the farmer has to sow and sow.
Nature is here to make us cheerful.

Adam Stoneman (10)
Oakhyrst Grange School

Bluebells

Bluebells, lovely and blue like a summer sky,
Live in the green woods,
Up with the breeze,
Even though I see some leaves.
Bluebells are wonderful,
Even though their shape is funny.
Life is divine,
Like all the world is shining,
So they are sun-loving jewels.

Emily Little (9)
Oakhyrst Grange School

Haiku

Beautiful fresh grass
Clear blue skies, holidays, *yes!*
I love summer, *hot!*

Thomas Dawson (8)
Oakhyrst Grange School

The Sound Collector

(Based on 'The Sound Collector' by Roger McGough)

A stranger called this morning
Dressed in dark green and red
Put every sound into a bag
'I've got them all,' he said.

The scratching of the mice
The clang of the broken clock
The roll of a dice
The bang of the door.

The clatter of the dishes
The hum from the tap
The splash of the fishes
The moaning of the baby.

A stranger called this morning
He didn't leave his name
He left us only silence
Life will never be the same.

Blanche Brown (8)
Oakhyrst Grange School

Summer - Haiku

Up above blue skies
Sizzling summer sunlight beams
Graceful birds up high.

Lauren Giles (8)
Oakhyrst Grange School

The Sound Collector

(Based on 'The Sound Collector' by Roger McGough)

A stranger called this morning
Dressed in blue and red
Put every sound into a bag
And his name was Ted.

The slam of the door
The rattle of the tap
The caw of a black bird
The tap of shoes.

The bang of the drum
The sound of the wind
The shout of my mum
The cry of a baby.

A stranger called this morning
He didn't leave his name
He left us only silence
Life will never be the same.

Oliver Clarke (8)
Oakhyrst Grange School

Shiny Summer - Haiku

Swaying, swishing leaves
Blowing wildly in the breeze
Birds soar up above.

Aman Mahi (8)
Oakhyrst Grange School

The Sound Collector

(Based on 'The Sound Collector' by Roger McGough)

A stranger called this morning
Dressed in red and white
Put every sound into a bag
And soon it will be night.

The ticking of the clock
The squeaking of the pen
The flapping of the book
The clucking of a hen.

The cutting of a blade
The clicking of a door
The scraping of marmalade
The tapping of a nail.

A stranger called this morning
He didn't leave his name
He left us only silence
Life will never be the same.

Michael Doble (8)
Oakhyrst Grange School

Summer - Haiku

Refreshing summer
Glows in the sky, shining bright
Always, the hot sun.

Rebekah Lindo (9)
Oakhyrst Grange School

The Sound Collector

(Based on 'The Sound Collector' by Roger McGough)

A stranger called this morning
Dressed in blue and yellow,
Put every sound into a bag,
He was a very ugly fellow.

The clang of the saucepan
The crunch of gravel
The bang of a tin can
The humming of a hummingbird.

The flapping of the curtains
The squeaking of a bed
The hum of a person
The snap of a lead.

A stranger called this morning
He didn't leave his name
He left us only silence
Life will never be the same.

Aimée Dyer (8)
Oakhyrst Grange School

Haiku

Bright sun sizzling hot
Birds soar through blue skies with grace
Orange sun setting.

Jack Bushell (8)
Oakhyrst Grange School

The Sound Collector

(Based on 'The Sound Collector' by Roger McGough)

A stranger called this morning
Dressed in red and pink
Put every sound into a bag
Do you think he winked?

The banging of the footsteps
The sizzling of the sausage
The miaowing of the cat
The creaking of the cottage.

The clatter of the toaster
The dripping of the tap
The chopping of the knife
The flapping of the cat flap.

A stranger called this morning
He didn't leave his name
He left us only silence
Life will never be the same.

Stefan Harper (7)
Oakhyrst Grange School

Summer - Haiku

Summer is sticky
Hot days dry up our water
Leaving cracks in soil.

Sam Lefevre (9)
Oakhyrst Grange School

The Sound Collector

(Based on 'The Sound Collector' by Roger McGough)

A stranger called this morning
Dressed all in red and green
Put every sound into a bag
And then a jar of beans.

The tick of the clock
The chop of the knife
The bang of rockets
The nag of a wife.

The clatter of the pans
The bark of the dog
The hum of fans
The scream of the wind.

A stranger called this morning
He didn't leave his name
He left us only silence
Life will never be the same.

Holly Macbeth (7)
Oakhyrst Grange School

Summer - Haiku

Sunflowers pop up
Hot sun shining in blue skies
Summer happiness.

Elizabeth Watmore (9)
Oakhyrst Grange School

The Sound Collector

(Based on 'The Sound Collector' by Roger McGough)

A stranger called this morning
Dressed in brown and blue
Put every sound into a bag
Is the stranger you?

The howling of the wind
The rustling of the leaves
The creaking of the railing
The flap of the trees.

The drip of the hosepipe
The splash of the swimming pool
The gush of the drain
The rattle of the tool.

A stranger called this morning
He didn't leave his name
He left us only silence
Life will never be the same.

Rebecca Phillips (7)
Oakhyrst Grange School

Summer - Haiku

Birds sing all day long
Horizon touches land, sea
Gold sun beams brightly.

Sean Tanner (9)
Oakhyrst Grange School

The Sound Collector

(Based on 'The Sound Collector' by Roger McGough)

A stranger called this morning
Dressed in dark blue and red
Put every sound into a bag
And carried them into bed.

The rattle of the door
The slam of the book
The creak of the floor
The jangle of the hook.

The clatter of the dishes
The drip of the sink
The gurgle of the fishes
He did that, I think.

A stranger called this morning
He didn't leave his name
He left us only silence
Life will never be the same.

Benedict Ruiz (8)
Oakhyrst Grange School

Haiku

The great green gardens
Give homes to small animals
Under cloudless skies.

Miles Stroud (9)
Oakhyrst Grange School

The Sound Collector

(Based on 'The Sound Collector' by Roger McGough)

A stranger called this morning
Dressed in green and brown
Put every sound into a bag
And carried them into town.

The miaowing of the cat
The click of the wardrobe
The rustling of my mat
The thump when I get into my bed.

The crashing of the door
The bang of the drawers
The clatter on the floor
The squeak of my toy mouse.

A stranger called this morning
He didn't leave his name
He left us only silence
Life will never be the same.

Sofie Spacey (8)
Oakhyrst Grange School

Summer - Haiku

Pretty flowers shine
People playing in blue seas
Birds tweet in bright skies.

Penny Durston (9)
Oakhyrst Grange School

My Special Stretch Limousine

My special stretch limousine,
Is quite a scene,
On the outside,
Bright pink and shiny,
On the inside,
Light blue and green.

The chauffeur called Bob,
Is great at his job,
Has a moustache dyed yellow,
And he always feels mellow.

As I wind down my window,
To see what's outside,
I see people staring,
Mouths open wide.

I smile at them back,
Waving as well,
As I ride in *my special stretch limousine,*
With pride!

Anna Gibson (10)
Oakhyrst Grange School

Summer - Haiku

Cool sparkling suncream.
Splashing waves over my feet.
Sunlight reflecting.

Benedikte Gibson (8)
Oakhyrst Grange School

The Young Lady From Spain

There was a young lady from Spain
Whose body was a real pain
So she went to the doctors
And he took her on a helicopter
And that was the end of the lady from Spain.

Christian Osei-Fosu (10)
Parish Church Junior School

Anger

Anger is like an exploding volcano
It sounds like a bomb that just went off
It feels like lava dropping on you
It smells like a crackling fire
It tastes like blood where a hole is in your tongue
It looks like a bull charging its enemy down
It makes you want to hurt others
Red represents anger
It makes you feel powerful
It knocks you down so you can't get up
It is the red Devil
Don't ever underestimate anger.

Kai Clack (10)
Parish Church Junior School

Man From Kent

There was an old man from Kent
Who wanted to build a tent.
It toppled, it turned,
The old tent burned.
The weird old man from Kent.

Michael Dewey (10)
Parish Church Junior School

The Starfish Day

I found a starfish on the bay,
I asked if it would like to play.
I took it home to show my mum,
The starfish said that it would come.
My mum said it was really rare,
When I told her on the top stair.
Now you have heard about that day,
I wonder if you'd like to play?

Stevie Lawrence-Wrist (10)
Parish Church Junior School

Blood Beast

What's that whining in the night,
It must be the creature with a terrible bite.
It flies through the air like a vampire beast,
It wants your blood for a midnight feast.
So hide your head, fold up your feet,
And tuck yourself under your sheet.
It'll get you in the end, wherever you go,
You can't escape from the . . .
Mosquittooooo,
Red ant.

Rachel Asafo-Agyei (9)
Parish Church Junior School

Flowers

The beautiful flowers, they grow every hour,
They give you a sense of pride to blow your mind.
The beautiful flowers, they smell as lovely as a rose,
They grow more when I spray them with a hose.
I add a bit of love and here come all the doves.

Gabrielle Dodoo (9)
Parish Church Junior School

Kane

Kane walks silently, hunting for his prey,
And suddenly it leaps but runs the wrong way.
Kane has a mane as bright as the sun,
It's as fluffy as candyfloss that children eat at one.

His teeth are as sharp as a razor for men,
He uses his teeth especially to eat a hen.
He has bright blue eyes which he closes at night,
He scares away creatures that are waiting to fight.

He goes down to the lake to get a drink
And whilst he's there he gives someone a wink.
So he goes for a walk in the long thick grass,
But you just have to remember he's not a trespasser.

Holly Wilson (10)
Parish Church Junior School

Above The Treetops - Haikus

Gorgeous and graceful
Soaring above the treetops
Amazing it is.

Resting on a tree
Looking at his creation
Then he starts again.

He stares at the moon
Hooting with passion, waiting
For his sweet freedom . . .

Hannah Bonam (10)
Parish Church Junior School

Football Crazy

My favourite team is Arsenal,
They are really great,
They always win matches,
They're not the team to hate.

Arsenal is the best,
They're better than the rest,
Their shirts are red and white,
They always drink Sprite.

Thierry Henry scores a hat-trick,
He's got a brother called Patrick,
He's so crazy about football,
Secretly what you don't know . . .
He's very, very lazy.

Alliyah Anmarie Thomas (9)
Parish Church Junior School

My Little World

I'm in my little world
And I'm very, very bored.
I haven't been myself,
I haven't followed the rules.
I'm trying to eat my toast
But I can't find the butter.
I'm asking where it is
But they all say I'm a great big nutter.
I'm trying to watch TV
I'm cheering and I'm clapping
Because it's all about me.

Dilara Sanli (10)
Parish Church Junior School

Foolish Bob

There was an old guy called Bob,
Who ripped off a brown doorknob.
He called the police,
To borrow their fleece.
The old guy called Bob.

There was a foolish guy called Bob,
Who never knew how to shut his gob.
He swallowed a balloon,
Made some cartoons.
The foolish guy called Bob.

There once was a fat guy called Bob,
He was a terrible old snob.
He had a very big belly,
Was also so smelly.
The fat guy called Bob.

There once was a footballer called Bob,
He did a terrible job.
He scored an own goal
And hit the pole.
The footballer called Bob.

Emmanuel Asare (9)
Parish Church Junior School

Dino Crusher - Haiku

Dino crusher walked
Along the bending pathways
Looking for his food.

Ryan Reakes (9)
Parish Church Junior School

Ten Top Reasons On How To Survive School

School is a very hard subject,
A very hard subject to do.
You get an A once, you get a B twice
Then you excel, *woohoo!*

10 Be number one, popular, cool.
 9 Remember you rule the school.
 8 Don't be a know-it-all.
 7 Score winning goals in football.
 6 Get picked first for a team.
 5 Don't be very, very mean.
 4 Know everything about everyone.
 3 Spend holidays in the sun.
 2 Have a packed lunch every day.
 1 Make sure you get an A.

School is a very hard subject,
A very hard subject to do.
You get an A once, you get a B twice
Then you excel, *woohoo!*

Omoyeme Akhigbe (10)
Parish Church Junior School

The Last Moment

All was silent
Dark and bitter
Not a single word to be heard in the street
A scream of fear
A howl in the wind
A whistle in the mist
A strike of lightning in the dark
The terrifying moment.

Lydia Asante (10)
Parish Church Junior School

Winter In The Park

It is cold, the air itself is ice.
You can hear the laughter of children
As they sledge down the snow-covered hill
Landing in a heap of joy at the bottom.
The frozen pond lay silent and still
As people glide across it wearing pointed shoes.
The bare trees sway gently and whisper quiet tunes to each other.
Parents trudge through a blanket of snow
Faces muffled into their scarves
Beckoning their children to come home . . .
All is now quiet . . .

Amy Hayes (10)
Parish Church Junior School

No-Brainers

There once was a guy called Ben,
Who had a new fountain pen.
He wrote on the walls
And on footballs,
There once was a boy called Ben.

There was a young man from Brazil,
Who had an old granny who was ill.
His uncle called Dan,
Who had a blue van,
That young man from Brazil.

There was a young man from France,
Who was very good at dance.
He ate a big cake,
And then caught a snake,
That young man from France.

Caleb Jordan (10)
Parish Church Junior School

The Last Moment In Time

As the mouse-catcher creeps
On its prey, it spots a swift wing
In the corner of its eye.
It now creeps on
It jumps and catches the angel arm wings.
As it is its last moment to live.

Nadia Ennani (10)
Parish Church Junior School

Me And My Dog - Walk

Walking my dog along
Whilst humming my favourite song
We passed a few birds
That seemed to be in herds
Whilst walking my dog along.

A day later, and it's on again
And we saw chickens locked on a chain
After that we saw,
A cat with a collar the size of a gong
All that whilst walking my dog along.

Later that day
Late, late into the night
Lou only wanted to play
Loop-the-loop toy, we held on tight
Latest walk we've ever done.

Kicking the ball whilst we walk
Killing ants with our feet
Killing time also with our talk
Kenny the beagle, we always meet
Kick of a time we have.

Maisie Lawrence (10)
Parish Church Junior School

My Nanny

My poor nanny
Lying there,
I don't know what happened
But now she's dead.

Still lying there,
With me crying my eyes out.
So upsetting,
Just wishing she was alive.

My poor nanny,
Her heart's not beating.
I keep wishing every day that she was alive,
Forever and ever.
Please Nanny, can you be alive?

Abigail Harris (9)
Parish Church Junior School

Diva Mums

There are diva mums
That always dance with their sons.
They dance till midnight
Till they squeeze them tight
And all that is left are their bums.

There are diva dads
That always go to the pub.
They always get drunk
Till they call people a punk.
Those old diva dads.

Callum Edgerton-Kirk (10)
Parish Church Junior School

Shirley Who Moved To Purley

There once was a girl called Shirley
Who one day moved to Purley
Then one day she had nothing to do
So she went on a trip to the zoo
There she met a bear
Who gave her a great big scare
So she ran to her home
Where she was alone . . . poor old thing!

Anna Cavallo (10)
Parish Church Junior School

Demon Cries

As we charged through into war
I knew that this would be the end
Even though we had armour of the strongest metal
The enemy was stronger than a million men.
I heard the cries of death of my closest friend.
I wanted to retreat, but I still thought about the death of families
and children.
I cut through thousands of men
But they seemed like demons being reborn.
All I wanted to do was bring peace to the world and my country.
I tried to stop and think but whenever I did,
Another demon would strike from behind or in front of me.
I looked for the strongest of them,
The one that kept bringing more of the demons.
In the end I saw my master go down, killed by one of the
furious demons.
I roared with anger and went straight for the leader,
Cutting through them like a T-rex running through a million-man army.
With one final roar I killed the leader of the demons.

Benjamin Kamara (10)
Parish Church Junior School

Funky Little Monkey

Funky little monkey running up the stairs,
Coming back down, eating tasty pears.
Funky little monkey running out the door,
Coming back in, then dancing on the floor.

Funky little monkey wearing underwear,
One hour later he's playing 'truth or dare'.
Funky little monkey playing with a ball,
Funky little monkey looks like a real fool.

Funky little monkey going for a whizz,
Funky little monkey doing his bizz.
Funky little monkey eating rats,
Funky little monkey licking all my cats.

Luke Owen Toh (10)
Parish Church Junior School

The Starfish

I saw a starfish in the bay
it had a very happy sway.

It sparkled with a lovely light,
it never gave me such a fright.

It's too divine and pearly white,
it could not keep out of sight.

It sparkled like a moonlit light,
I practised fish games in the night.

Rianna Richards (10)
Parish Church Junior School

People I Met

I went to Peru

There was a young boy in Peru
Who wanted to buy a shoe
Expensive they were
With polar bear fur
Shed fresh from the London Zoo.

I went to Argentina

A woman in Argentina
With the name of Celina
Bought a bag
Made from stags
Then went to a football arena.

I went to England

There was an Englishman
Who lived in a Coca-Cola can
He got drunk
And kicked a monk
Then was transferred to a pan.

I went to Brazil

The old evil man in Brazil
He had the right to kill
So he got a knife
And stabbed his wife
And had to pay the bills.

I went to Mexico

The clever girl in Mexico
Who loved to act in shows
It was her dream
Just to be in a scene
The clever girl of Mexico.

These are the people I've met across the world!

Christopher Joseph Do
Parish Church Junior School

Figure Skating

You can do it on ice,
You can do it on snow,
You can do it practically
Everywhere you go.

You can do it in a dream,
You can see it on TV,
You can do it with your eyes shut,
Well, so it seems.

But you'll have to practise,
If you do not,
Your brain could end up,
In a very tight knot.

(PS so could your legs!)

Lydia Kosonike Akaje-Macauley (10)
Parish Church Junior School

Swift Wing

Gliding swiftly through the tree bark
Swift Wing spots prey.
Shooting, silently, dodging giant tree barks
He aims at the prey and . . .
The spear-shaped beak jabbed the prey.
With a ruffle and a squeak,
A magnificent dust storm,
Lay dead the enormous prey
And stood still the proud, tall,
Paper-white Swift Wing,
Now sipping softly, the prey's
Glistening red, tasty, blood.

Jasmin Elizabeth Winifred (9)
Parish Church Junior School

The Silly Man From Hong Kong

There once was a man from Hong Kong
Who loved to drink tea all day long.
It gave him a pain
But he did it again
The silly man from Hong Kong.

Josie Ibitoye (10)
Parish Church Junior School

Elements

Blazing orange,
Rising streaks of red,
Forked tongues.
Columns of flame,
Untouchable.

Cool and transparent,
Rippling and sparkling,
Slippery and blue,
Crashing and foamy,
Unstoppable.

Green and bushy,
Great towers,
Old and crinkly,
Bare and isolated,
Unpredictable.

Howling, bitter,
Cloud pusher,
Warm breeze,
Ever-flowing,
Invisible.

Emily Shadbolt (10)
Parish Church Junior School

The Unheard Cry

The gentle sob
The quiet whistle waving,
Dead leaves crunched,
Her last word frozen in the air . . .

Olawunmi Akanji (10)
Parish Church Junior School

The Wonderful Colours

White is the colour when snow is falling,
Yellow is the colour when the sun is happy.
Black is the colour when God is angry
Brown is the colour of a sad tree.

Billy Thompson (10)
Parish Church Junior School

The Blue Kangaroo

There once was a blue kangaroo
That slept for a moment or two.
Alas, while he napped
The hammock string snapped,
And he fell on a startled gnu.

Sarah Langhorne (10)
Parish Church Junior School

The Fat Cat's Hat

There was once a very fat cat,
Who wore the most beautiful hat.
The boy had a toy
And the fish had a dish
But nothing as beautiful as the Fat Cat's hat!

Heather Gibbs (10)
Parish Church Junior School

My Best Friends

L ikes to make people laugh
A lways wants attention
U nhappy when left out
R eady to always play
A lways likes to cheer people up
J oking all the time
A lways likes to focus on her work
D ances when she feels like it
E nds games with lots of fun

R eliable (very)
E nthusiastic in sports
A lways positive (always)!

M athematic and always helps
A mbidextrous (writing with both hands)
L oves playing with animals
A lways helpful to others
I ntelligent, especially in maths
K ind to almost everyone
A ngry inside when she gets things wrong!

Hannah Mwebeiha (9)
Parish Church Junior School

The Starfish

I found a starfish in the bay
When I went swimming yesterday
Starfish, starfish in the ocean
Moving along in slow motion
Many arms and colours bright
Sea stars are a special sight.

Machaela Prendergast (10)
Parish Church Junior School

The Fight Of The Devil

The skull-crusher crushes the enemy,
The bodies all around of the Earth-livers.
The owner of the skull-crusher holding it like a volcano
With his face like red-hot lava.

The skull-splitter splits his enemy down the middle.
The gunfire all around with his heart booming
Like a bell with his face like red-hot fire.

Tommy Marsh (10)
Parish Church Junior School

Friends

Friends look after you,
When you go boohoo.
They may even take you out
They won't make you shout.

Friends encourage you
And play with you too.
They do the right thing
And makes you want to sing.

Tameka Gowan (9)
Parish Church Junior School

There Once Was A Girl

There once was a girl called Milly
Who unfortunately was silly
She bumped her head
Fell right into bed
And woke up decidedly chilly.

Susan Mohammed (10)
Parish Church Junior School

Space - Tanka

Stars gleaming so far
The blazing sun so immense
So small to so big
Planets from the universe
Wow! It is so amazing.

Krystal Clark (10)
Parish Church Junior School

That Poor Little Kangaroo

There once was a kangaroo,
that wanted to get out the zoo.
So he tricked the keeper and done a leaper
at last he was free from the zoo.

So this brave little kangaroo
that hopped all the way out the zoo
Had bumped into a bee
that was hovering by a tree.
The bee turned around and
made a buzzing sound.
It stung him on the back
so Kanga gave it a smack.
That brave little kangaroo.

That poor little kangaroo
whose back was sore, boohoo
He had no treatment
and no power for leapment.
So he hobbled back to the zoo
that poor little kangaroo!

Hannah-May Reid (10)
Parish Church Junior School

The Weird Man

There was a weird man from Kent,
Who always slept in a tent.
Then one night he went out
And to the roundabout
And that was the weird man from Kent.

Charlie Coker (10)
Parish Church Junior School

My Best Friends

L aughs a lot
A lways happy
U n-ending happiness
R eady to play, even if she's hurt
A lways kind

J oking all the time
A lways focused
D epended on a lot
E ndless fun time

H appy as always
A ngry hardly ever
N ice (I need to think of a better word)!
N ever-ending joyfulness
A lways kind
H armless

M y funny friend Hannah M

R eally kind
E ndless playtime
A lways positive too.

M y best friends.

Malaika Nwankpa (10)
Parish Church Junior School

Jake

There once was a boy called Jake
Who ate an enormous cake
Reading a book
He saw a cook
And threw him into the lake.

The next time I saw Jake
He was just about to bake
He started to frown
Then jumped up and down
That's my weird friend Jake.

Jake was very silly
He hurt a girl called Dilly
She ran away
And wasn't seen the next day
But Jake ran off with Billy.

Again I saw poor Jake
He was dressed up as a snake
He slithered around
All over the ground
But everyone knew it was fake.

Jumping off a plane
We saw Jake again
Down he fell
Off to Heaven with a girl
He said goodbye again.

Laurence Ben Johnston (10)
Parish Church Junior School

Trophies 'N' Medals

Trophies come in all different shapes and sizes,
and are used for first place prizes.

Winners love to get them
but losers want to forget 'em!

Medals you win in an Olympic Game
when you're usually on your way to fame.

There are three different coloured medals: bronze, silver and gold,
which anyone would be proud to hold.

Trophies for the football leagues are the best
proving your team's better than the rest.

Then you flip up your top
and the wine cork goes *whizz! Pop!*

Trophies 'n' medals come in all shapes and sizes
and are used for first place prizes.

Joshua Aidan Elliott (10)
Parish Church Junior School

Me!

H ard-working (only at maths)
A ngry at people who annoy me (my little sister)
D isco diva (won ten trophies)
J ealous of people (who win competitions)
E njoying myself (laughing)
R iding my bike every day (or twice a day).

Hadjer Boumazouna (9)
Parish Church Junior School

The Girl In Pink

There once was a girl dressed in pink,
Who always made the boys wink,
Then when she went to a disco,
She danced to hip-hop with co
As she boogied on down to the floor,
The boys shouted out . . . *'More!'*

One morning her hair,
Was completely unfair,
She went to school,
She found out she wasn't cool,
So the boys ignored her
And called her . . . *'Sir!'*

The next morning she woke up
And said, 'What's up?'
Then went to school
And found out she *was* cool,
And took her friends to the mall!

Kenya Barnett (9)
Parish Church Junior School

My Friends

K ind and loving
E ndless laughter
N ever sad
Y ou can always rely on her
A lways ready

H elpful and kind
A lways loving
N ever selfish
N ever greedy
A lmost always worrying
H elpful to others.

R eminding.

Rhianna Rock (10)
Parish Church Junior School

The Young Man Called Aaron

There was a young boy called Aaron
Who had a teacher called Mrs Barrron
She cried and she cried
For there was nowhere to hide
From that naughty young boy called Aaron!

Aaron Bennett-Jordan (10)
Parish Church Junior School

Summer

Summer has begun.
Adults and children alike wake up to the ever-expanding sun
Streaming through every window.
All the children have their scrumptious breakfasts and then . . .
The fun begins.

Children begin to escape from their parents,
A lot of them meet together,
Then they turn on the sprinklers,
Others go swimming,
Maybe some go on bike rides.
Millions of events happen through these wonderful and freeful days.

These events in the day slowly but surely slow down to a
                                    relaxed fashion,
Of watching cricket,
While having a brilliantly made drink
And having the smell of a wonderful barbecue in your nostrils.

Finally the day comes to an end,
While the children in their beds are itching for another
                                    exciting day ahead.
Everyone has enjoyed this and they are looking forward to the next.

Sonny Cott (10)
Parkside School

The River

The young river starts its life high up
in the majestic mountains of the north,
where the air is clear and cold and the
wind whips through the air fiercely.

As the excited water bubbles and gurgles
its way around the grassy banks,
it plays around like a youthful child.
The river seems anxious to discover
what lays around the next corner.

The fast-moving water gushes down in a hurry,
twisting and turning its way past trees and
lowland hills.

In time, its banks broaden and its pace slows
as it begins to mature.
The water's flow becomes gentler and it begins
to meander this way and that as the river,
now moving more slowly, continues its onward
journey towards the sea.

It takes ever broader turns as the water relentlessly tries
to work its way southwards towards its destination.

The river seems wider too, it is now reaching maturity,
it seems sleeker and wiser, no longer in such a hurry
but enjoying its journey as it winds through the fields
where horses graze on the grass, contentedly and small
children play noisily in the fields around its banks.
Sometimes they throw sticks into the river and race the water
for a while.

The river struggles to keep on going as its power begins to wane,
it broadens in size and its twists and turns grow longer
as it flows past the draping trees.

The river now seems like an old man as it approaches the sea,
its final destination;
It rounds the last bend in its long journey and flows into the sea,
its waters joining with the salty seawater and merging into one.

Michael Woolston (9)
Parkside School

What Is The Sun?

Sun is a yellow rubber duck
floating in the air from cloud to cloud.

Sun is a light bulb in the sky
lighting up faraway places.

Sun is a very shiny coin, at the end
of the rainbow in a pot of gold.

Oliver Mould (10)
Parkside School

Cricket

It's a . . .
Hard hitting
Fast running
Quick bowling
Six smashing
Glory riding
Crowd stunning
Stadium filling
Pressure building
Game!

Oskar Kolk (10)
Parkside School

The Rocket

Up in the air
I am 2,000 ft.
It is very high
Nearly to the moon
But not that high.
Then I go in a flash
Sprinkling to the ground.

Ben King (10)
Parkside School

River

It is a sunny day and everyone is going to the river,
Some people are fishing, some people are having a picnic,
And as the sun goes down, people are leaving
But people are going for a walk.

Charles Hibbert (10)
Parkside School

Cracking Cricket

The Oval is full with critics,
The crowd clap the batsman in dramatically
The batter takes middle,
The bowler bowls.
The ball is slammed along the green grass for four.
The cluster of people clap dauntlessly.

The same bowler bowls the third over,
It is a fabulous bowl
But the batsman is going to make mincemeat of it.
Suddenly, with the sound of a gunshot,
The ball is hit.
Glamorously the airborne ball soars through the sky,
The scarlet ball clears the boundary tremendously.

On the last over it is all tense,
The ruby-coloured ball flies through the mix of gases.
The ball hits the crease and smacks the stumps.
They fly out of the ground like they are rockets taking off!
The bowler shouts, 'Howszat!'
The umpire puts a finger up,
The bowling team cheer and they win the ICC Cricket World Cup!

Harrison Lee (10)
Parkside School

BBQ

The smoke is released,
The barbecue has started,
The meat is sizzling,
The heat is scorching.
I can hear the scratching
Of the grill.

The food is divine,
I need to combine
The ketchup with the meat.
My dad didn't give me any leek,
My mum looks chic,
She starts to shriek.
She sees a mouse
On her blouse.

When the barbecue is over,
We play baseball, I hit a big
Dad's still eating like a pig.
I smashed the ball
Oh no, I'm caught!

William Payne (10)
Parkside School

Frogs

I am a frog and I like to jump,
Jump to each lily pad
And jump, jump, jump!
I like springy ones
What do you like?
I am a frog and what are you?

Louis Broomfield (9)
Parkside School

What Is Frost?

Frost is a kilogram of sugar
blowing from place to place.

Frost is some iced milk
waiting to melt.

Frost is steam from hot water
going cold in winter.

Frost is a thousand diamonds
twinkling in the winter grass.

Andrew Howorth (9)
Parkside School

BBQ While Fishing

The rock pool
Was a big round ball,
The summer breeze was like a wave against the sand,
The sizzling was like a band.

When I caught a long fish,
Mum put out a dish,
I drank some cool Coke,
When there was thick smoke.

The fish was like a rainbow,
And Dad's dough
Was shaped like a bow.
It was fun,
Trying to bake Dad's bun.

The sunset came,
The mixture of the colours blended so well,
Our eyelids started to droop then fell.

Edward Grove (10)
Parkside School

Days At The Beach

Days at the beach are most memorable,
The sun standing proud like a lion,
Shining through the sky.

Building a sandcastle is very tiring,
Trying to keep the roaring waves from attacking.
Having to defend your precious kingdom,
But finally, the waves triumph.

Skimming stones,
Trying to find the best flat stone
To skim,
Trying to beat your record.

Ice cream, vanilla, honeycomb,
Strawberry, raspberry and chocolate,
Every flavour imaginable,
Everyone refreshing.

Sunbathing,
Letting the sun heat you up
Like a microwave.
Tanning you, the hot sand relaxing you.

Finally bringing a portable barbecue onto the beach,
Eating the fish you caught this morning
Finishing the day with a lovely piece of fish!

Oliver Haines (10)
Parkside School

The Best Days Of My Life

I came back home from my last day of school,
In our metallic black car.
I go past a tall round house.
I smell the smell of freshly cut grass, *mmmmm!*
I now know it is summer!

When I get home I do my holiday homework.
When I've finished I am so excited I run a mile!
Then I do all the things I couldn't do,
Playing ping-pong against the wall, bowling with my family.
After the summer I feel very manly.

Renny Smith (10)
Parkside School

Majorca

The sun is a melted coin,
In a blue purse,
If I walked up the stairs
I'd burn to a cinder without a care.
Perfect silence everywhere,
Not even a bird to sing.

There is a freezing sprinkler over there,
I see a bear next to a river,
The river is like a sparkling pool of blue
And the bear is a fur ball jacket that you wear.

I hire a boat,
Then I wrote
This poem of Majorca,
The island of Spain.

Oliver Dunn (10)
Parkside School

America

I flew into America,
We were driven to the hotel,
It was as hot as a barbecue,
As the sweat sizzled off my skin,
Oh, glorious America.

I walked into my first
Theme park of the day,
The smell of popcorn and ice cream,
Oh, fantastic America.

I jumped into the pool,
It was as warm as the sun,
I joined water fights
And played water polo
Oh, awesome America.

I walked into Fenway Park,
We sat down to see the
Red Sox vs the New York Yankees
Oh, radical America.

Max Kerslake (11)
Parkside School

Never Disturb The Dinosaur

I am a dinosaur who likes to kill
I am a heavy sleeper.
I have claws to catch my prey
And I have teeth as sharp as knives.
To rip out their bones and spines.
But when I've eaten all of that
I go right back to sleep.

Charlie Crook (9)
Parkside School

Summer

In your garden,
You may see
Things that are
Not to be.

Colourful flowers
Here and there
Sunsets which
Are everywhere.

Running through grass
Without any brass,
I move quickly,
My brother is almost bare,
Without a care.

Running through
Fields of harvest hay
And then I run
Towards the bay.

I'm so hot
I could drink a lot
Of water and possibly,
A small amount of beer!

I run through waves,
While the boy misbehaves
I drink some seawater.

Towards the end
Of my day
I start to head
From the bay.

Summer is over,
I cry and cry
Along comes autumn,
Leaves on the floor
Goodbye summer!

Adam Welby (10)
Parkside School

Thorpe Park

Thorpe Park is a smashing place in the summer,
With water rides and gentle rides,
People with ice creams, looking at the scenery,
All the people looking in awe
When a lion roars.

Adults and kids in the pool
And babies in the paddling pool,
Rides are gleaming
And people are screaming.

Stealth is high,
A bit too high,
When the people go on Tidal Wave
When the boat comes down the people at the bottom get wet.

People doing deals
And families eating their meals,
Some people on the roller coasters, upside down
And crows look down.

Colossus is big!
And scary.
Stealth goes up to the sky,
Now I know it is 303 feet high!

Dominic Wood (10)
Parkside School

Summer In Dorset

Dorset I find one of the hottest places.
You have to pack some very big cases.
I love BBQs on the beach at night.
I hope there aren't any fights.

The heat blazing on my back,
The suncream I just happen to lack.
Swimming in the sparkling sea.
Just makes me want to pee.

When the sand is in-between my toes
I completely forget my lows.
I love the summer.
But when it ends it's a bummer.

Harrison Moore (10)
Parkside School

Party

I like parties in the summer nights.
Chocolate fountains and fizzy drinks.
Music and the PS3 on the big TV.
The barbecue flaming and eating the darkness away.

The DJ jamming on with the music on.
Talking to my friends and playing on the Wii
Playing some footie and cricket as well
Getting some cold drinks to cool you down.

Strawberries tasting so sweet.
Having some chocolate and different meat.
The swimming pool all heated and light.
That's why I love parties in the night.

Freddie King (10)
Parkside School

Holiday USA

USA sucks on the Interstate,
pick-up truckers rule the Texas state,
I get to the hotel, everything's alright,
Surround system is on all night.

In the pool I beat up brov
but he fights back with a slash
Dad comes in, we down him with a splash
I am grounded because brov's a brat.

We have to go to the mall, great
I walk into the shop, I go straight to the models
I see a Porsche Carrera GT
so I plead with my dad so I don't waste my cash.

Christopher Addison (11)
Parkside School

BBQs In The Summer

Sizzling sausages on the BBQ,
The hot searing sun shining down on you
Smoky cheeseburgers with onion and BBQ sauce.

Hanging out with your friends and family of course,
And on the trampoline it's really fun
When I go flying but I get hurt.

After the BBQ
We have a massive water fight
And everyone gets soaked
And my mum has a right go at me.

Alex O'Brien (10)
Parkside School

Cricket

The bowler bowls the ball,
Batter swings at the ball,
Batter misses the ball,
The bails fall down,
I love cricket.

The bowler bowls the ball,
Batter swings at the ball,
The ball goes in the air,
Slip catches the ball,
I love cricket.

The bowler bowls the ball,
Batter swings at the ball,
Batter slugs the ball,
It's a six,
I love cricket!

Charlie Horne (11)
Parkside School

Gold

Brightly, gloriously, now the sun
Strides into the day, his job to be done.
The town awakes to its shine,
Trees sway and streams race to another bright day
The sun sees all good and evil,
The flowers yawn open
And then,
As darkness creeps closer,
The sun retreats for another day.

James Hibbert (11)
Parkside School

Football On The Beach

Football on the beach!
I went and bought a peach!
The blistering sun flashed down on my face!

Playing on the beach with my mate!
The next one who comes is my date!
The sizzling sun on our feet!
This is a real treat!

The same song playing by the ice cream man.
'Oh I wish he'd play some jam,'
Said my mate Sam.

Matthew Szepietowski (11)
Parkside School

Summer Fun

The daffodils are gone,
so are the tulips.
Spring has passed,
but summer is here!

Cricket in the park,
tennis on the courts.
The hot sun beating down,
run for the shade!

The sea is warm,
let's go for a swim.
Or put on your sunscreen,
and lie on the sand.

There's lots of ice cream,
strawberry, chocolate and vanilla.
And these are just a few reasons
why summer's the best!

Harris Asher (11)
Parkside School

Ice Cream

I went to a beach
My mum gave me a peach.
I wanted an ice cream!
My mum just gave me a suncream.

Toffee and chocolate, my favourite flavour
But before, I had to do a favour
While doing it, I saw children begging
But the parents didn't buy them, then they were crying!

I like the way it cools down.
It feels like it is a crown!
With the ice cream, everyone has laughter
The end of the story is probably 'happily ever after'!

Brian Ryu (11)
Parkside School

Cricket In Summer

The fielders are doing well in their job,
Especially the new kid called Bob.
I love the cherries on the bat,
It really goes with the fielder's hat!

I see the ball spin to the wicket,
You've got a check-it!
Then the suncream bursts in the air
And some of the patches of grass are bare.

The crowd goes wild over a four,
But it only went on the floor.
Suddenly the players scream because of a catch
And I guess that's the end of the match!

Nicolas Stolz (11)
Parkside School

Holiday

I love the holiday times
There are lots of things to do.
Shooting, playing football,
I don't know what to do.

I'm going to play cricket now,
I'm the best in the team,
I hit the ball
It goes up in the air, it's a six!

The end of the holiday is near
I'm running out of time,
I sit here doing my homework
Dreaded school is nearly here.

Hugo Solway (11)
Parkside School

Untitled

Puff up the pillows
Pull up the covers
Sleep goes fast
Time goes past
As if it was only a second
Have a nice rest

If you can't sleep
Listen to music or a story tape.

Oscar Ferguson (10)
Parkside School

Theme Park

On a scorching summer's day,
I rode my red bike,
With blue racing stripe,
To the devilish theme park.

First I flew across the park
On number three of the top ten thrill coasters!
As shocks of fright shot up my spine,
In the creepy ghost train,
On the way out of the train
I stopped at a café.

I took a trip down the big drop,
Falling down two hundred feet in a log-shaped boat.
Splash! Water flew everywhere as I came out soaked!
I whipped out a towel and dried myself.

Getting ready for Colossus!
The fastest of them all,
Top of the chart.
I entered the cart,
Awaiting the start.
It was great!

It was time to leave,
I left the park with amazing memories,
I just can't wait to tell my friends,
It was the best day ever.

Brandon Koen (10)
Parkside School

The Queen

The cool blue throne stood waiting.
The queen was coming.
Her gown was pure white silk, like the rising moon.
Her diamond eyes fitted her majestic head perfectly.
The crown of feathers displayed her power and might.
Her subjects were clearly under their queen's spell.

She glided seamlessly and her steps were light.
She paddled in the azure water causing ripples as she swam.
The river too was under her magic spell.
The queen was a swan swimming in the serene water
Her faithful subjects followed.
They were still hypnotised by her.

Her journey ended when she reached her green palace.
She entered the palace of greenery, longing to see her children.
The queen's subjects waited, pushed away by the guards.
They stood staring at the emerald palace.
Although their queen was no longer in sight, they stayed.
Her spell was still at work.

Inside was small, but not poorly decorated.
Paintings with golden frames hung on the wall.
Beds with quilts as red as roses stood silently.
The queen went to wake her children.
They wore long silver outfits, just as beautiful as their mother.
The queen was home, where she wanted to be.

Julia Parison (11)
St Hilary's School, Godalming

Happiness!

Happiness looks like a room full of people having fun.
It sounds like a band singing a song of joy.
It smells like a beautiful rose petal swaying in the breeze.
It tastes like a sweet chocolate cake, tender and soft,
                                        melting in your mouth.
It reminds me of those happy days a long time ago.
And it feels like a warm fiery home in a cold scary place.
Happiness is like a rainbow, all multicoloured.

Michael Griffin (9)
St Hugh of Lincoln Catholic Primary School, Woking

Anger

Anger is red like burning lava and your heart is fading away.
It smells of sweat and smoke.
It sounds like exploding bombs.
It feels like your head is going to burst.
It reminds me of an erupting volcano.
It tastes like rotten banana skins!
It also feels like an earthquake about to split the ground in half.

Michael Chapman (9)
St Hugh of Lincoln Catholic Primary School, Woking

Feelings

Anger is like hot lava bursting out of a volcano,
Love is like a beautiful pink rose petal drifting in the air.
Fear is the colour of black when you can't move yourself.
Happiness is the colour of bright yellow when you can
                                always see where you're going.
Hate smells like a burning fire of riches.
Sadness smells like a rotten egg.

Emily Bullen (9)
St Hugh of Lincoln Catholic Primary School, Woking

Love

Love feels like a soft rose petal floating away
Love sounds like a soft wind blowing
Love is very loving and caring like a child and mother hugging together
Love smells like a juicy red apple
Love is happy like a patterned butterfly flying in the sky.
Love is red like a poppy flying away.

Megan Louise Avery (8)
St Hugh of Lincoln Catholic Primary School, Woking

Hate

Hate is the feeling of nightfall,
Hate is normally near,
Hate smells nasty,
Hate is in your ear,
Hate is as black as a storm,
You'd better stay away,
Hate is wicked,
It might come to you one day,
Hate is bad,
It's crackling and flickering,
It tastes of red-hot chilli peppers.

Sophie Hubbard (9)
St Hugh of Lincoln Catholic Primary School, Woking

Hate

Hate feels like the sun fading,
Hate looks like the setting sun,
It smells like porridge,
It tastes like fish oil gleaming,
It sounds like screaming in my ear.

Daniel Naughton (8)
St Hugh of Lincoln Catholic Primary School, Woking

Anger

Anger is red like burning lava and your heart is fading away.
It smells of sweat and smoke.
It sounds like exploding bombs.
It feels like your head is about to burst.
It reminds you of a volcano erupting.
It tastes like rotten banana skins.
It's like you going to jump about screaming.

Charlie Ruiz (8)
St Hugh of Lincoln Catholic Primary School, Woking

Sadness

Sadness smells like a fresh summer breeze
In the morning and tweeting birds calling for help
And a burning fire coming up to the sky.

Sadness looks like a field of beautiful flowers
And a tree falling upon you
And shadows all around.

Sadness feels like a cold breeze touching your skin
And the sun is slowly wearing off
And the clouds are slowly closing and it is getting dark.

Georgia Quigley (9)
St Hugh of Lincoln Catholic Primary School, Woking

Fear

Fear is grey and dull like a lonely room in a house
that nobody lives in.
With a garden that looks like it goes on forever and ever.
Fear tastes like disgusting food.
Fear sounds like somebody screaming loudly in your ear.
Fear feels like ghosts creeping up on you and starting to scare you
like a nightmare that seems everlasting.

Thomas Vardy (8)
St Hugh of Lincoln Catholic Primary School, Woking

Fear

Fear feels like the ground shaking.
It makes you remember when you got lost.
And makes you feel as if you have been hit by a hammer.
Your heart is pounding very fast.
Fear is like your blood running from your head to your toes.
Fear is like a shadow scaring you.

Niall Runswick (9)
St Hugh of Lincoln Catholic Primary School, Woking

Love

Love is like a pink rose petal drifting to the ground.
Love smells like a fragrance from a beautiful perfume.
Love feels like a soft feather floating in the air.
Love tastes like sweet chocolate in your mouth.
Love is the colour of a red rose in a bright flower garden.
Love sounds like a bluebird singing sweetly.
Love reminds me of a little chick with its mother.

Alice Ketteringham (9)
St Hugh of Lincoln Catholic Primary School, Woking

Sweet Love

Love feels like happiness
So when you meet the right person it comes out like a feather.
Love tastes like sweets and strawberries ripening in the sun.
Love smells like Mum's cooking.
Love reminds me of sweet flowers.
Love looks bright pink.

Alyssa Charlotte Promnitz (9)
St Hugh of Lincoln Catholic Primary School, Woking

Fear

Fear smells like a dark, dusty room.
Fear looks like an empty playground full of ghosts.
Fear sounds like somebody creeping up on me.
Fear tastes like a cold cherry ice cream.
Fear reminds me of people dying in a movie.
Fear feels like people kidnapping me.

Samuel Robinson (8)
St Hugh of Lincoln Catholic Primary School, Woking

Love

It smells like a rose full of fragrance,
It tastes like a chocolate cake melting in my mouth,
It sounds like beautiful music flowing through my ears.
It reminds me of happy times playing with my friends.
It feels like a soft, fluffy pillow lying on a bed.
Love looks like a beautiful flower swaying in the breeze.

Rory Kelly (9)
St Hugh of Lincoln Catholic Primary School, Woking

Happiness

Happiness is as bright as an angel,
Happiness is the feel of soft feathers,
Happiness is the taste of sweet maple,
Happiness is lovely,
Happiness is as fab as a pale pink rose flowing in the breeze,
Happiness is lovely,
Happiness is a sign of hot summer sun on your knees.

Estelle Harland (8)
St Hugh of Lincoln Catholic Primary School, Woking

Love

Love feels like an emotion inside you.
It tastes like a warm chocolate chip cookie melting on a summer's day.
It looks like a cute puppy staring at you.
Love isn't a jumping, crazy thing.

It is a delicate, soft, caring, nice, never-let-you-down thing.
It's an ice cream cone just melting away.
It's a whole bunch of red roses given to you by your dream date,
Love is a velvet blanket lying on top of you when you sleep.
Love is so important to us - it really is!

Niamh Ryan (9)
St Hugh of Lincoln Catholic Primary School, Woking

Anger

Anger is red like a pool of boiling hot lava.
Anger tastes bitter like an unripe plum.
Anger looks like a volcano about to erupt.
Anger sounds like the heavy beat of a drum in my head.
Anger feels like a red-hot iron burning in my hand.
Anger smells like the smoke from a fresh bonfire.
Anger is burnt orange like a fire.

Billy Peacock (8)
St Hugh of Lincoln Catholic Primary School, Woking

Happiness

Happiness is as bright as an angel.
Happiness is the feel of soft feathers.
Happiness is the taste of sweet maple.
Happiness is lovely.
Happiness is as fab as a pale pink rose flowing in the breeze.
Happiness is a sign of the hot summer sun on your knees.
Happiness is great!

Isabela Maria Ramanath (8)
St Hugh of Lincoln Catholic Primary School, Woking

Love

Love tastes like a juicy red apple hanging from a tree.
Love sounds like a gentle wind blowing a fluffy cloud away.

Love looks like a happy child clinging with his sticky
hands to his mother

Love smells like a ripe succulent strawberry
sitting on some lime-green foliage.

Aimee Cook (8)
St Hugh of Lincoln Catholic Primary School, Woking

Fear

Fear feels like your heart is falling through your body,
Fear smells like cold darkness,
Fear sounds like a rushing storm flying past,
Fear tastes like a cold ice cream in the winter.

Connor McLean (9)
St Hugh of Lincoln Catholic Primary School, Woking

Hate! Hate!

Hate feels like everybody's fading away,
It looks like the world is collapsing,
It smells like smoke burning your heart,
It tastes like fish and my hopes being crushed.
Hate reminds me of anger and pain,
It sounds like screaming in my ear.
The colour of hate is red and yellow.

Joshua Jones (9)
St Hugh of Lincoln Catholic Primary School, Woking

Fear

Fear is the colour of tramps' dull clothes, ripped and torn.
Fear is the sound of people screaming in despair.
Fear has the taste of a million shouts rushing down my throat.
Fear smells like an old spirit floating through a haunted house.
Fear looks like a family with no love.
Fear reminds me of people everywhere, with no one to love
and care for.

Aoife Coyle (10)
St Hugh of Lincoln Catholic Primary School, Woking

Laughter

Laughter is yellow like a flickering torch.
Laughter sounds like birds and chipmunks chittering with the
whistle of the wind.
Laughter tastes like soft, creamy ice cream covered in Brazil nuts.
Laughter smells like candyfloss turning in the sticky, sugary bowl.
Laughter looks like melted chocolate freezing in an icy fridge.
Laughter feels like warm custard slopping over a tart.
Laughter reminds me of my friends.

Adam Hayton (10)
St Hugh of Lincoln Catholic Primary School, Woking

Hate

Hate is red like a crackling fire on a cold winter night.
Hate sounds like a hurricane blowing trees over onto the pure
spring grass.
Hate tastes like the blood on your fingers after you've killed a calf.
Hate smells like burning plastic in a boiling pan of water.
Hate looks like lots of trees swaying violently in the wind.
Hate feels like anger flowing through your veins.
Hate reminds me of when I've had painful times in my life.

Anastasia Murphy (9)
St Hugh of Lincoln Catholic Primary School, Woking

Hate

Hate sounds like a shivering cold whisper in my ear.
Hate is black like a black widow crawling up my throat.
Hate tastes like bitter herbs dipped in poisoned blood.
Hate smells of gas there only to kill me.
Hate looks like Hitler in my nightmare.
Hate feels like a sharp blade piercing my skin.
Hate reminds me of war destroying friendship between countries.

Elliot Samuels (10)
St Hugh of Lincoln Catholic Primary School, Woking

Silence

Silence is as white as a huge polar bear on top of snow.
Silence sounds like someone is creeping up on you, but all you
                                        can hear is your heartbeat.
Silence tastes like ice cream mixed with fresh strawberries.
Silence smells like a fresh summer's morning.
Silence feels like being scared because someone is creeping
                                                up on you.
Silence looks like shadows are creeping up on you but you don't
                                        know where from.
Silence reminds me of the calm air.

Allyson Varndell (10)
St Hugh of Lincoln Catholic Primary School, Woking

Silence

Silence looks like the morning sun.
Silence is crystal-clear like a diamond ring.
Silence smells like an unpicked, scrumptious cherry.
Silence tastes like a crispy apple in the morning sun.
Silence looks like a warm bath with chocolate everywhere you look.
Silence feels like the touch of a cold winter night.

Charlie Kaine (10)
St Hugh of Lincoln Catholic Primary School, Woking

Darkness

Darkness is black, the colour of loneliness.
Darkness sounds like an owl hooting in the middle of the night.
Darkness tastes like misty air on a winter's night.
Darkness smells like fresh snow on a cold winter's morning.
Darkness looks like a warm, creamy mug of hot chocolate.
Darkness feels like a freezing cold bath.
Darkness reminds me of things I have lost.

Chloe Foster (10)
St Hugh of Lincoln Catholic Primary School, Woking

Happiness

Happiness is yellow like the sun's blazing shine.
Happiness sounds like a twinkling star shooting past you in the
great big sky.
Happiness tastes like a great sweet sugar fizzing in your mouth.
Happiness smells of warm chocolate melting in front of you.
Happiness looks like a great pot of friendship.
Happiness feels like a bright soft touch of a soft cushion.
It reminds me of the happiness of my dog.

Hannah Randall (10)
St Hugh of Lincoln Catholic Primary School, Woking

Fear

Fear is black, the colour of black spiders.
Fear sounds like screaming and screeching at night.
Fear tastes like scares from a ghost from night to day.
Fear smells like blood dribbling from a jaw at night.
Fear looks like a frightened face from death.
Fear feels like a scary castle in the night.
It reminds me of being in bed and hearing noises.

Jasmine White (10)
St Hugh of Lincoln Catholic Primary School, Woking

Happiness

Happiness is yellow like a cheesy, smiley face.
Happiness sounds like the chatting of schoolgirls in a
                                        screaming playground.
Happiness tastes like ruby-red strawberries dipped in warm,
                                        melted chocolate.
Happiness smells like toffee popcorn on a cold winter day.
Happiness looks like two butterflies floating through the breezy air.
Happiness feels like the soft shiny fur of a newborn puppy.
Happiness reminds me of my family!

Ella De Vivo (9)
St Hugh of Lincoln Catholic Primary School, Woking

Hate

Hate is the colour of roses, thorny red roses.
Hate is the sound of screams, cold, high-pitched screams.
Hate tastes like blood dripping from your jaws.
Hate smells like gas burning on a stove.
Hate looks like faces, burning red faces.
Hate feels like being bitten, bitten by a shark.
Hate reminds me of gunshots shooting through the air.

Jaime Miranda (10)
St Hugh of Lincoln Catholic Primary School, Woking

Darkness

Darkness is black like a spider spinning a web.
Darkness sounds like a cat screeching on a cold winter night.
Darkness tastes like the cold winter moonlight.
Darkness smells like the cold frost sprinkled with chillies
                                        on a spring morning.
Darkness looks like a midnight forest.
Darkness feels like an abandoned Jumbo Jet rusting away
                                        with creepy-crawlies in it.
Darkness reminds me of a loss in my family.

Ryan Fernandez (10)
St Hugh of Lincoln Catholic Primary School, Woking

Fear

Fear is the colour of the black night with the shadows of trees.
Fear sounds like a screaming girl running from a vampire's son.
Fear tastes like a sweating wolf and sour blood from a fox.
Fear smells like a rotten egg being eaten by a skunk.
Fear looks like your blood spurting out, your family is dying and
you pass out.
Fear feels like werewolves and crows.
The world is ending,
End of creation has begun and no one can stop it.
The moon has gone, the sun has gone,
The Earth is left to fear the end of creation
And everyone can fear the end of the Earth.

Alexander Frow (9)
St Hugh of Lincoln Catholic Primary School, Woking

Fun

Fun is the colour of a rainbow
on a wet, drizzling day.

Fun is the sound of
joy and laughter.

Fun is the taste of a steaming
cup of hot chocolate on a frosty
winter morning.

Fun smells like marshmallows
melting in your mouth.

Fun looks like children playing
in wide-open fields.

Fun feels like excited children
on Christmas Eve.

Fun reminds me of having
a good time with your friends.

Darius Mohepat (10)
St Hugh of Lincoln Catholic Primary School, Woking

Fun!

Fun is the colour of a bright juicy orange on a small tree,
Fun sounds like small children giggling and laughing,
Fun tastes like soft, fluffy pink candyfloss,
Fun smells like chocolate melting in a warm glass bowl.
Fun looks like fluffy white bunnies hopping in a big green field
Fun feels like a soft bouncy ball sitting on the pavement,
Fun reminds me of friends and family playing and talking
together happily.

Sophie Stevens (10)
St Hugh of Lincoln Catholic Primary School, Woking

Darkness

Darkness is black like a creeping, crawling spider.
Darkness sounds like a hooting owl in the dark night.
Darkness tastes like a misty clear air on a winter's night.
Darkness smells like a burnt ruined house.
Darkness looks like a big hairy bug climbing up a wall.
Darkness feels like you're in the loneliest place.
What does it remind you of?
Darkness reminds me of loss.

Katie Naughton (10)
St Hugh of Lincoln Catholic Primary School, Woking

Laughter

Laughter is green like a fresh new tree,
Laughter sounds like children getting tickled, non-stop!
Laughter tastes of cream oozing for delight,
Laughter smells of a freshly baked potato.
Laughter looks like fun, please join in, let's run.
Laughter feels soft and delightful.
Laughter reminds me of people enjoying their previous lives.

Jay Mearns (10)
St Hugh of Lincoln Catholic Primary School, Woking

Laughter

Laughter is yellow and orange like a dancing candle on a cold winter's night.

Laughter sounds like a tinkling bell from an ice cream van.

Laughter tastes like strawberries ripened in the summer sun.

Laughter smells like freshly cut grass in the morning dew.

Laughter looks like a tiny kitten suckling from its mother.

Laughter feels like warmth and love.

Laughter makes me remember all the happy times I've had.

Nicola Turner (10)
St Hugh of Lincoln Catholic Primary School, Woking

Fear

Fear is the colour of green oak trees.
Fear sounds like someone's footsteps running and then a laugh.
Fear tastes like bitter lemons, left far too long.
Fear smells like dead rotting bodies.
Fear feels like blood dripping down.
Fear reminds me of when my cat was born and I saw it.

Charlie Watson (9)
St Hugh of Lincoln Catholic Primary School, Woking

Fun

Fun is yellow like the flickering sun.
Fun sounds like joy and happiness on a hot summer's day.
Fun tastes like banana ice cream in a crystal clear bowl.
Fun smells like freshly washed bedcovers on a cold winter's night.
Fun looks like children picking daisies from an open field.
Fun feels like sitting on a sofa made of chocolate.
Fun reminds me of playing hockey with my friends on
the concrete ground.

Thomas Buckland (10)
St Hugh of Lincoln Catholic Primary School, Woking

Happiness

Happiness is like a fire flickering in the wind
Happiness sounds like laughter in the air.
Happiness tastes like cold, dripping ice cream
The touch of happiness is like a heart pumping
Happiness feels like a burning heart waiting to come out
Happiness smells like a new, fresh, soft mattress in a shop.
It reminds me of people skipping happily in the day.

Shannon Phillips (10)
St Hugh of Lincoln Catholic Primary School, Woking

Silence

Silence is pure white like when you are trapped and all alone
Silence sounds like plain nothing, when everyone's around you
but you can't hear anything.
Silence tastes like dry air being forced down your throat,
Silence smells like freshly cut grass in the wind.
Silence looks like a clear wine glass with a stain of
pure lipstick on the rim.
Silence feels like you have no one and nothing to care about you.
Silence reminds me of when everything is still and you
can hear or see nothing.

Georgia Blanco-Litchfield (10)
St Hugh of Lincoln Catholic Primary School, Woking

Anger

Anger is red like a tightly balled fist.
Anger is the sound of screaming and shouting
                              in the silence of the night.
Anger tastes like ruby-red blood.
Anger smells like a fire ready to get bigger.
Anger looks like the Devil roaming round your mind.
Anger feels like a pain stabbing right through you.
Anger reminds me of friendship.

Sophie Cawkwell (10)
St Hugh of Lincoln Catholic Primary School, Woking

The Sun

Glistening, burning,
Glittering turning.
Heat on my back, bright in my eyes.
Dazzling in the clear blue skies.
Casting shadows, beams of light,
No sign of shade until the dark of the night.
Gleaming cherries, rich, ripe berries.
The sun glares down upon my neck,
Scorching it until it is red.
Then when it sets, a vibrant light glows,
And all the Earth is still . . . asleep!

Isabel Turner (11)
St Hugh of Lincoln Catholic Primary School, Woking

Wind

It started . . .
Blowing across bleak deserts,
Crashing against ancient waves,
Controlling life and growth,
Claiming the attitude it craves.

The wind has spoken.

The wind is always around us,
Calm, strong, passive, aggressive.
It will rule the world forever,
It's in charge.
It's possessive.

The wind will be a source of energy
For the future,
A power, a force,
One force to be reckoned with . . .

Thomas Ketteringham (11)
St Hugh of Lincoln Catholic Primary School, Woking

Rainbows

Red is for love
That's sent from above,
Orange is for comfort,
Like a loving thought,
Yellow is for times of happiness.
Like at a party in my best dress.
Green is for jealousy,
As I look at pretty Lily,
Blue is for peace,
As a white dove whistles.
Indigo is for hatred,
The worst feeling you can have.
Violet is for calm,
While people do no harm.

Emma Higgins (10)
St Hugh of Lincoln Catholic Primary School, Woking

Ice Cream

Ice cream is cold and creamy
It melts softly in your mouth
What's your favourite flavour
Chocolate or strawberry?

You can get all kinds of ice cream
Fabs, Cornettos, crunchy cones
Magnum, Galaxy or even 99 Flake.

Ice cream comes in different shapes and sizes
One scoop, two scoop can be done
Three scoop, four scoop is enough!

Emily Randall (11)
St Hugh of Lincoln Catholic Primary School, Woking

Emerald Express

At six in the morning I get out of bed,
I eat, wash and get dressed.
I get in my car, driving to my destination
Which, as always, is the train station.
I meet my cousin whose name is Jess,
And we get on the Emerald Express.
The Emerald Express is a train
That goes from London to Spain.
As you might know it's emerald-green.
Its shiny carriages are sparkling clean.
At the conductor's whistle, it thunders away
Into the night or into the day.
It shouts *'Choo-choo!'* as it whizzes past.
It's just a blurr, it goes so fast!
It puffs out smoke, it puffs out steam,
It's very smooth - like in a dream.
It leaves on time, it's never late,
Swift and elegant - it's great!
So I say to you, from me and Jess,
The best train of all is the Emerald Express!

Rosie Byers (11)
St Hugh of Lincoln Catholic Primary School, Woking

Secrets

Secrets are nice and secrets are fun
Secrets are bubbly and shine like the sun!
Secrets are silent and should be whispered with care,
Secrets are friendly, for close ones to share.
Secrets are golden and secrets will stay,
Like a burning passion that will not go away.
Secrets are private and secrets are personal,
Kept safely under lock and key,
Secrets are private and personal,
Are private and personal to me!

Samantha Love (11)
St Hugh of Lincoln Catholic Primary School, Woking

God's Creation

The sky is as black as an onyx,
The moon and stars are like diamonds in the sky,
The sea is like sapphire,
The sea creatures are swimming in the sea.

The sun in the morning is a topaz
With the birds flying gracefully in the sky.
The grass and trees are like emeralds.
Children playing peacefully
And this is God's creation.

Daniel McNulty (11)
St Hugh of Lincoln Catholic Primary School, Woking

Friends

Friends are forever!
You can count on them
And depend on them
Or can you?
Friends are treasures
Like the ones that lie
On the bottom of the sea.

Your old friends are gold
Your new ones are silver
You might fight about things
That are not important
But forgive and forget
Otherwise you might regret.

Friends are important
Look after them.

Ciara Sullivan (10)
St Hugh of Lincoln Catholic Primary School, Woking

The Wonder Of A Duck

(Inspired by 'Cat Began . . .' by Andrew Matthews)

It took the softness of a feather and a smooth wall
and made its body.

It took the roughness of bark and the roughness of
a thistle bird and made its wings.

It took the voice of a whistle and took the sound of a
butterfly and made its voice.

It took the shape of a cone and the fall of snow falling
and made its beak.

It took the orangeness as a pen and the straightness of a stick
and made its legs.

Now the duck was made.

Emma Cooper (11)
St Hugh of Lincoln Catholic Primary School, Woking

Tina

Tina sleeps when she is tired
She sleeps all over the house
When she's awake she plays in the garden
Hunting for a bird or a mouse.

Tina is soft and cuddly
Cute in every way
She sometimes gets muddy
But she's always home every day.

Tina can be very fierce
When anyone gets in her way
Her scream is like a pierce
Everyone knows who's the boss around here.

Ryan Quigley (11)
St Hugh of Lincoln Catholic Primary School, Woking

Happiness

Happiness is warm and soft and silky.
Clean and smooth.
It shines in the sun,
Gold, yellow, bright and happy.

Happiness makes people smile and laugh,
Builds up friendships
And makes the whole world shine
Like a brilliant place.

Everyone has happiness
Deep down inside.
People just need to find it
In their heart.
Because happiness is one of the
Greatest things on Earth!

Ellen Verrier (10)
St Hugh of Lincoln Catholic Primary School, Woking

What Are Friends?

Friends always stick up for you
But they always tell the truth
If you are fighting
They always forgive you

Friends always share everything
And they never leave you out
They always protect
And they also care

You get understood by friends
They help you through troubled times
They will never mock
They respect instead.

Alice Langley (11)
St Hugh of Lincoln Catholic Primary School, Woking

Three-Headed Dog Began!

(Inspired by 'Cat Began . . . ' by Andrew Matthews)

Three-headed dog began . . .
He took the glisten of the stars,
He took the shape of the ball,
He stole a button off a shirt.
Then the three heads of the dog were made.

He stole the body of the tiger,
He took the softness of his fur from a
Feather out of a comfy pillow.
Then his body was made.

He took the strength of a metal pole
Then his legs were made.

He stole the shortness of a water bottle,
Then he took the fluff from a piece
Of furry material.
That made his tail

Then the three-headed dog was made.

Nicola Hayes (11)
St Hugh of Lincoln Catholic Primary School, Woking

Cars

Cars are cool to drive.
They look very fast.
My dad's car is black.
It is a BMWX5.
It looks very cool on the motorway.
It can go 175mph.
Cars are very helpful
Because they take you around the town and city
And place to place in the town.
My mum's car is a BMWX3!

Reece Power (11)
St Hugh of Lincoln Catholic Primary School, Woking

My Cat

My cat has a brown tail,
And her miaow is as loud as a wail,
She miaows at your feet,
When you come in from the street,
Her fur is as soft as the finest feather,
Even when it's bad weather!

Catching a mouse,
Catching a woodlouse,
Razor-sharp claws,
And silky soft paws,
Pink-white nose,
White feather-soft toes.

Sleeping all day,
At night she finds her way,
All through the woods,
Sees Robin Hood,
Comes back home,
And is as hard as stone,
Up she goes
To Heaven's home.

Jessica Martino (11)
St Hugh of Lincoln Catholic Primary School, Woking

Water

Water is refreshing as
Ice cream on a summer's day
Water is delicious as a
Roast dinner on a Sunday
Some people long for cold Coke
Some for icy lemonade
But . . .
I can't wait till this lunchtime
To have a drink of water.

Stephen Frangiamore (11)
St Hugh of Lincoln Catholic Primary School, Woking

Untitled

(Inspired by 'Cat Began . . . ' by Andrew Mathews)

He took the wings of a dragon
He took the air from the sky
and his wings were made

He took the fire of a devil
He took the air of an eagle
and his fire was made

He took the body of a gorilla
He stole the climbing ability of a monkey
and made his body

He took the fangs of a lion
He took the strength of a bread knife
and made his teeth and fangs

He took the hands and legs of the gorillas
He took the nails of a thousand people
and made his hands and legs to climb

He took the sight of a hawk
He took the air of an eagle
and his eyes were made

He took the nose of a gorilla
The nostrils of a lion
and his nose had been made.

Gorilla - Checker-Kong was done.

Alex De Piano (11)
St Hugh of Lincoln Catholic Primary School, Woking

Friends

Friends are like the best thing that has ever
happened to you,
You can always depend on friends
and trust them.
Friends are like a breath of fresh air.

Friends are love and they will always
share things with you.
Friends are planes, they will carry you up.
Up and away to another place.
Friends are like family and family always
Comes first, before ourselves.

Friends are that shining star you always see at midnight,
And you will always be together forever.

Charlotte Smith (11)
St Hugh of Lincoln Catholic Primary School, Woking

Ice Cream

It is a variety of colours
And flowers,
There are many different types,
Some melt in your mouth
And some you have to bite.
It is always cold
So put it in the freezer,
Otherwise, it will be liquid
And might make a mess!

Nicholas Haley (10)
St Hugh of Lincoln Catholic Primary School, Woking

My Special World

My special world
Is a place full of fun
It's a great place
To leap and run

It has dragons and monsters
Horses galore
Unicorns and Pegasus
Snakes slither on the floor

I can be the horse
With my hooves a-raising
Or the great griffin
My colours blazing

I can have friends right there
Mostly from TV
Even if they're a kind of mutant
Nobody can see

I can see them at
Any time
In the class
Or outside.

Sometimes I get
A bit too far
I whinny and roar
In class or car

My special world
Is a place that never ends
But it is only complete
With your favourite friends.

Hannah Baron (11)
St Hugh of Lincoln Catholic Primary School, Woking

A Summer's Day

In the summer I have to say
I love to watch the green grass sway.
The sun beats down on the joyful Earth,
We've enjoyed the sun since our birth.

Everyone rushes to the sea
While I sit in the shade of a large tree,
The sea sparkles under the sun,
Then I know the evening's begun.

Then I laid my head for the night,
Waiting for the morning light.
Then the sun fades into the night's sky,
Then I realised the day has just flown by.

Hannah Brierley (10)
St Hugh of Lincoln Catholic Primary School, Woking

There's A Monster Under My Bed

There's a monster under my bed,
It's small, dark and hairy.
To my mum I said,
'It's big, black and scary.'
I swear it has some wings,
To get halfway up the book case
And steal all my things.
Including my old brace
In the school,
I found out it was real,
The boys think I'm a fool,
But there is a monster under my bed.

Terry Dullaghan (11)
St Hugh of Lincoln Catholic Primary School, Woking

The Wind

The wind can be warm
The wind can be cold
The wind can be strong
The wind can be as sharp as knives.

The wind can blow you off your feet,
The wind scares cats so their hair is static.
The wind frightens the dogs with their tails between their legs
The wind, the master of the Earth.

Kevin Heath (11)
St Hugh of Lincoln Catholic Primary School, Woking

Moonlight Dance

When the sun goes down and the moon appears
I look out the window and give out a cheer
For now the world is no longer bright
I can finally begin my dance in the moonlight

Down the stairs and out the back door
Skipping down the steps to the place I adore
The grass glistens from leftover rain
The moon and the stars are my friends again

I now lose myself as I begin my dance
From beginning to end, I stay in a trance
Below the moon and stars is where I belong
Gracefully dancing forever long

I dance through the streets and the park
Silently dancing throughout the deep dark
Not the wind nor rain could prevent my fun
I dance in the moonlight but never in the sun

I can never be as happy as when I'm dancing alone
Whether warm or cold never whisper or a moan
I finish my dance on the velvet of the lawn
And return to my room at the hint of the dawn.

Kristi Stone (11)
South Farnham Junior School

Space Pirates

You've heard of pirates and you've heard of spacemen,
But have you ever heard of a cross between them?
They're called the space pirates and cor they're a bunch,
If you get them angry they'll eat you for lunch!
They plunder the universe in a spaceship-like boat,
And to stop them from doing this there's no antidote,
When they attack they're not very nice,
After all their motto is 'mince, slice and dice',
So if you do see a weird-looking spaceman,
Start running or your life will go down the pan!

Nicholas Bailey (10)
South Farnham Junior School

Martin Luther King Rap

Martin Luther King
Never did a thing -
Wrong!
All his life long.

Believed in this one dream
To make white people less mean,
Chipping away at the laws
To stop racist wars!
He was a great man,
I am his number one fan,

Then he was shot,
But people never forgot -
Him!

It was the world's biggest sin.

James Overington (11)
South Farnham Junior School

In The Stables

In the stables the horses neigh
In the stables I get covered in hay
In the stables I saddle up the horses
In the stables they get three courses
In the stables we polish the tack
In the stables bridles go on the rack
In the stables the ponies get rugged
In the stables the ponies get hugged
In the stables we wash their tails
In the stables they drink pails and pails!

In the field the horses chase
In the field they race and race
In the field they gallop in circles
In the field they are as graceful as turtles
In the field horse rear and buck
In the field we find shoes of luck
In the field ponies eat the grass
In the field they live first class
In the field we clear out the poo
In the field, ah, I need one too!

In the sand school ponies canter and jump
In the sand school we land with a bump
In the sand school we ride up the centre line
In the sand school we have a race against time
In the sand school we trot over poles
In the sand school horses fall in the holes
In the sand school our instructor tells us off
In the sand school ponies drink from the trough
In the sand school we do a shallow loop
After my lesson I go home for soup!

Megan Barnett (11)
South Farnham Junior School

My Puppy!

Small, mini, tiny
She is part bat
Small, mini, tiny
Some mistake her for a cat

She runs like a cheetah
Her hearing is precise
She likes to eat meatah
But she's scared of even mice

Small, mini, tiny
She is part cat
Small, mini, tiny
Some mistake her for a bat

When she is hungry
She will even have your hand
When someone's at the door
She'll bark louder than a marching band

Small, mini, tiny
She is part bat
Small, mini, tiny
Some mistake her for a cat

Once we had a gerbil
He was very small
Then Holly got hold of him
Now there is no gerbil at all

Small, mini, tiny
She is part cat
Small, mini, tiny
Some mistake her for a bat

Woof, woof, woof
Woof-woof, woof-woof-woof.

April Young (10)
South Farnham Junior School

Fruit

Orange, yellow
Red and green
The brightest colours
I've ever seen

Apple, mango
Pineapple too
Pears and passion fruit
I like these too

Strawberry-red
Shaped like a heart
Some are sweet
Others tart!

Oranges round
Bananas green
Only they're not ripe
If they were I'd be keen

Clementines, satsumas
Kiwis and plums
They taste so nice
I can taste them in my gums

They taste nice in pancakes
Oh, sweet lemon
You have it for pudding
Strawberries and melon

Fruit is so nice
Give it a try
Oranges and apples
Go on, go buy!

Amy Ball (10)
South Farnham Junior School

Questions

Why is the world round?
If I lie sideways will all of my organs slide sideways too?
Why is the sky blue?
Why are we here?
What is my future like?

Really? No! When?
How? Why?
It couldn't?
She didn't!

But . . .
If . . .
Is . . .

Questions questions
Nothing but questions!

Who was the first king or queen?
Why is 'happy' called happy and 'sad' called sad?
Who invented Mother's Day?
Is the answer to two plus two really four?

Really? No! When?
How? Why?
It couldn't?
She didn't!

But . . .
If . . .
Is . . .

Questions, questions
Nothing but questions!

Freya Jefferys (11)
South Farnham Junior School

Dragons, Creatures Of The Sky

Dragons,
A great, but feared beast,
Untameable, but able to be friendly,
Thought of as a monster,
But could be a saviour,
Dragons, good or bad?

Dragons,
Strong, but swift,
They come in many shapes and sizes,
Their scales unbreakable,
Sharp teeth,
Wings large and powerful,
Their eyes shining with light or evil,
Dragons strong and swift.

Dragons,
Move strongly or quickly,
They fly so swiftly,
They could crush a thousand boulders,
Their fiery breath could burn down cities,
It could be heroic,
They control their actions.
Dragons.

Charlie Cowles (11)
South Farnham Junior School

My Fancy Dress Party

Spider-Man in the living room trying to catch flies,
The Fantastic Four are leaving, they're just saying their goodbyes.

Popeye is here, he's on the pond and sailing,
I know the banshees have arrived, I can hear them wailing!

Van Helsing went up the stairs holding a big stake,
Oh golly, I really hope the vampires are awake!

There's Superman who is making mischief with a mop,
There's Wonder Woman on the landing in her bright red top.

Batman's on the doorstep he's the last one,
Robin's already inside, enjoying all the fun!

Later the dancing stopped, the music died away,
That was a great party I had today!

Beatrice Morris (11)
South Farnham Junior School

My Pony Dancer

My pony is my favourite mammal,
She is much better than any camel,
She lives at my house
And is as quiet as a mouse,
Her name is Dancer,
But she likes being called Prancer,
Although she's as fast as a cheetah,
She is a very good eater,
I'm never lonely,
I have my pony.

Elana Whistlecroft (10)
South Farnham Junior School

My Two Cats

In my house we have two cats,
One called Foxy, the other called Fluff,
One is stripy, the other one's not,
They both chase mice,
But Mum's had enough!

Birds, mice, insects and all,
They're in the bedrooms and in the hall,
They may have to go, but not too soon,
She thinks next-door's dog is just a loon!

Thomas-George Murray (10)
South Farnham Junior School

Secret Thoughts

I have a magic box which contains
Thoughts, ideas and games,
So when I'm bored,
I look inside,
Where my ideas hide,
Which stretch from mountain to mountain five million metres wide,
My box is now too small,
Oh goody here they come every one and all.
Some of fire-breathing dragons that puff out smoke,
Sunny days on the beach with strawberry ice cream,
Fears of being eaten by a great white shark,
Diving with dolphins,
Standing under a red, green, yellow, blue, violet, indigo and orange
dazzling rainbow.

Hollie Atkins (11)
South Farnham Junior School

The Scarecrow

When no one is around
He creeps around the allotments
Birds zoom off when they see him
Twigs snap under his feet
When the scarecrow comes alive!

His old hat balanced on top of his straw-stuffed head
Soil-covered straw comes out of his body
You can tell something's happened
When the scarecrow comes alive!

All the plots are covered in prints
The ones with bushes that were once tidy
Are all upturned in the morning
When the scarecrow comes alive!

No one really knows what's happened to their lovely allotments
They try to protect them with fences
But it never works
When the scarecrow comes alive!

Now I know what happens to people's carrots, lettuces, raspberries
Strawberries, potatoes and tomatoes
When the scarecrow comes alive!

Thea Foxwell (11)
South Farnham Junior School

Stuff

Every Monday when I go into the classroom,
My teacher asks me what I did at the weekend,
I say, 'Stuff.'
She says, 'Well you must have done something exciting,
Stuff is not a very good word to use.'
I say, 'Yea, I suppose so.'

One Monday, as usual, she asked again, expecting to hear the usual,
I stood up straight in front of her,
And I said . . .

'Well, I went into my garden and played with the fairies,
It was amazing, they were very pretty and I liked them very much,
I have also made best friends with the fairy queen.

Then I went back in time to the Victorian ages
And met Charles Dickens for a cup of tea,
He is a very nice man and I would like to see him again soon.

Oh, and you will never guess what happened,
I went to the park with some friends and I saw a man-eating frog,
So really it was a very exciting weekend, Miss.'

She looked like she didn't believe me
And, the strangest thing is,
She hasn't asked me what I did at the weekend
Since that very Monday.

Briony Turton (11)
South Farnham Junior School

Chocolate

Chocolate is my favourite food,
It's rich and creamy and tastes so good!
There's milk, there's dark and white as well,
There's a lot of chocolate, I'm glad to tell!
Chocolate doesn't just come in cubes,
It's made in truffles and creamy tubes.
You drink it as hot cocoa and have them as lollipops,
You can buy every chocolate shape in all of your local shops!
Chocolate is creamy, runny or thick,
A lot of chocolate you buy on a stick.

So many chocolates are just divine,
Some people just eat it to pass the time!
My favourite's milk chocolate, I don't know about you,
There are so many things that chocolate can do.
Chocolate on a doughnut, is what I've tasted
And chocolate ice cream, which cannot be wasted.
Chocolate cake is one of the best,
It's often used at an important fest.
The smell of chocolate is just so great,
I share my chocolate with my best mate!

What I really long for is a chocolate fountain,
With chewy marshmallows, piled in a mountain!
Or juicy strawberries, that'll be good,
Chocolate is obviously the number one food!
It's wrapped around biscuits and that is nice,
I prefer chocolate to a big bowl of rice!
When the smell of chocolate drifts by my nose,
It smells much better than my stinky toes!
Everybody knows that chocolate is good,
And I am fond of it as it's my favourite food!

Megan Jones (10)
South Farnham Junior School

The Match!

My dream's come true
I can't believe I'm here
Standing in Old Trafford
My team so very near
So many people round me
All singing for 'The Devils'

Across the stand the opposition
Will take the song to many levels!

Here my team comes running up the tunnel
Followed by the enemy
Who hopefully we'll pummel
Whistle blows, they start to play
A ball to Saha, but no here comes Andy Faye!
No, stop, wait, what's going on here?
A cross from Giggs to Rooney
And suddenly everyone's going looney!

Goal they scream!
1-0 to United
2 minutes later the whistle blows
Half-time is here
Players run off faces all aglow.

Second half starts
Only 45 minutes till the end
Scholes passes to Carrick
But Young defends
What's happening now?
A penalty awarded
Ronaldo steps up
It's a goal, finally we're rewarded!

2-0, 2-0 the United crowd chant
We're going to win, we're going to win
The others surely can't!
It's over now and we have won
Boy, oh boy, that was so much fun!

Thomas Hodgson (11)
South Farnham Junior School

Tea For Two In The Arctic

When polar bears have their nightly dine,
Oooh, I must say, it is very fine.
Their white furry coats sit at the table,
Buried in the snow - they are very stable.
When they prepare
Tea for two in the Arctic!

For the birds it's a different story,
Stealing the fish, they have all the glory.
They swoop down and grab the things,
The fish giving their last little screams.
When they prepare
Tea for two in the Arctic!

The seals are the most interesting of all,
Swimming streamlined in the icy pool.
They slide back on their bellies with their prey,
Yelping and barking all the way.
When they prepare
Tea for two in the Arctic!

So when you have your next tea,
Please remember with brilliant glee,
The animals who have prepared,
Tea for two in the Arctic!

Nicole Williams (11)
South Farnham Junior School

What Do Vampires Eat For Lunch?

What do vampires eat for lunch?
Lizards, insects, bones to crunch?
For starters do they suck your blood
Followed by beetles covered in mud?

Then they go on to their second course,
Cockroach soup with hairs of horse,
Toad in the hole (I mean what I say!)
What do you mean you don't want to stay?

Livers of rat and bit of seal,
This is what I call a real meal!
A bit of meat to make the stew,
Human eyeballs, just a few,

Rabbits' ears and foxes' tails,
Sharks' teeth and guts of whales,
Just to remind you, this isn't a potion,
Come on in and join the commotion!

Now for the best part, worm delight,
Just think of it now, what a sight!
So what do you think vampires eat?
Come on in and take a seat!

Amy Lubach (11)
South Farnham Junior School

The Haunted House

The creaking of the floorboards,
The crooked pictures and old swords,
Doors hanging off their hinges
As I'm walking my shoulder twitches.

Faded walls covered in cobwebs and dust,
Some leftover food and a bit of a crust,
I swept the dust from the floor,
What did I find? A trapdoor.

I tugged at the door, but it wouldn't budge,
I didn't run, I decided to trudge,
The windows were black, no light shone through,
There was nothing in sight except an old shoe.

I turned the corner and there I could see
Two bulging eyes staring at me,
I sprinted away, watching the floor,
I turned the corner but where was the door?

Chloe Jones (11)
South Farnham Junior School

Crab

I am a crab, I live on the shore,
got hard pincers not soft paw;
I snip and nip if you get in my way,
or if I am having a bad day,
I zigzag across the sands,
to escape children's hands,
that is why you should watch out,
we don't like to mess about,
I am a crab!

Lauren Dockerty (11)
South Farnham Junior School

The Candy Shop

Sweeties and chocolate all in a row
All of the jars have ribbons or bows
Cadbury's or other, make up your mind
Percy Pigs are so hard to find

Rhubarb and custard, the sweetest of all
They all disappeared to the village hall
There are milkshakes and lollies all set to go free
Spiders and sheep and a big bumblebee

The candy man stands holding a sign
Selling the sweets all in a line
With toddlers and children and teenagers too
He stands selling cows going *moo, moo, moo, moo*

It's really sad when it's time to go
I didn't buy my cow but I called it Moe
As we step through the door, we all get let down
But then we have fun shopping in town.

Rosie Booth (11)
South Farnham Junior School

Can You Guess?

Great mover,
Wild flicker,
Easy pusher,
Wonderful zapper,
Amazing linker,
Eye gripper,
High number,
Mad zoomer.

Answer: A TV remote control.

Sophie Richardson & Georgia Morton (9)
The Chandler CE Junior School

Global Warming

Thick-smelling smoke,
Toxic, dark car fumes,
Come,
As the race begins,
Electricity,
Good for making light,
But why not use the sun?
Plastic bags,
Trying to rot,
But only slightly succeeding,
While letting off unwanted gases
Into the universe.
Tall incinerators,
Burn, burn, burn,
Black, black, black,
But should all this happen?
If no one recycles,
If no one walks,
If no one stops all this,
I am doomed.
You are doomed.
Everyone is.
Everything is.
But all anyone cares about,
Is money.

Kate MacLachlan (8)
The Chandler CE Junior School

Imagine

Imagine there were no words.
Would there be instructions for top secret plans?
Would we know the lines for an act
Or would we have to use sign language?

Imagine that we had no noses.
How would we breathe
When we're enjoying our favourite Sunday roast?
How would you engross yourself in sweet-smelling flowers?

Imagine if we had no machines.
You would not be able to rest
While the washing's being cleaned!
You could not relax and watch TV.

Imagine there was no global warming.
A waste-free planet,
With not a sign of pollution or waste,
Everything spotless or recycled.

Imagine no oxygen.
Would we evolve and breathe carbon dioxide?
Would we be extinct?
Would we have to create oxygen?

Imagine no world.
Would we need a new planet to live on?
Would we just float around in outer space?

So many questions and yet none of them answered.

Harry Osborne (9)
The Chandler CE Junior School

Bogey

My finger went up my nose,
It went up and up,
I pulled it out,
There was something green on the end of my finger,
It was a bogey!
As quick as a flash I stuffed it in my mouth,
It tasted of sour apple,
I spat it out,
No! I had spoiled my work.
The teacher came,
She looked at my work with a puzzled face.

Abi Bolton (9)
The Chandler CE Junior School

Kennings

High singer,
Deep swimmer,
Fin flapper,
Food scrapper,
Boat toppler,
Mood mapper,
Bridge maker,
Water sprayer,
Milk feeder,
Bad seer,
Silent ruler,
Breathing cooler.

Answer: A whale.

Hannah Barnett, Charlotte Clarke (8) & Rhiannon Davies (9)
The Chandler CE Junior School

Earth

Earth crumbles,
like a devastating avalanche,
triggered by something more forceful than lava.

An impenetrable substance,
even by a burst of
air with a poisoned bite.

A wave of cunning water
couldn't weave a path through this
God-like material.

Luminous beams of light
will not be able to penetrate
this legendary thing.

The darkest night could
not freeze its blessed bones
to a fatal halt.

One hundred jabs from a
frost king's spear of ice
would not drive it crazy.

Even a divine element,
 mystic beyond belief,
would be as light as a feather touch.

Only cruelty in its purest form
would demolish this fuel's
hunger for everlasting life.

Robin Benjafield-John (9)
The Chandler CE Junior School